FAREWELL, DUBLIN,
BUT NEVER GOODBYE

FAREWELL, DUBLIN, BUT NEVER GOODBYE

Donal McKenna

The Pentland Press Ltd.
Edinburgh · Cambridge · Durham

First published in 1992 by
The Pentland Press
5 Hutton Close
South Church
Bishop Auckland
Durham

ISBN 1 85821 011 9

Typeset by Spire Origination, Norwich
Printed and bound by Antony Rowe Ltd., Chippenham

To my wife, Norah

Contents

Foreword

It is always a very considerable pleasure to be able to assist, even in the smallest possible way – as in writing this Foreword – a family historian who has the knowledge, commitment and most of all patience to write a story about his family and to get it published. This pleasure is greatly increased when the author is a member of the Family History Society of Cheshire of which I am currently Chairman.

This is a biographical story which includes, as the author himself states, warts as well as beauty spots. The narrative is fast moving with the intimate detail that only an ex-Officer of the Merchant Service and an Irishman would be able to tell.

It would of course spoil the enjoyment of this work to elaborate any further on that point other than to say, simply, that the story starts in Dublin, includes expulsion from a Convent, stories of Batchelor's Walk in that fair City, as well as stories based in the Mediterranean around Iraq and in Japanese Girl Houses . . .

Peter D. Dewdney

Chapter One

The morning was unexpectedly warm and the child within Cait's swollen belly was very active, its legs kicking every which way indicating that it was anxious to be born. She had slept little and as a result she felt exhausted; sitting on the edge of the bed, she set about massaging her stomach with olive oil. Although this would be her second child, she was only twenty-three and concerned that the telltale stretch marks of motherhood should be minimal.

Her husband, Sean, stirred across the bed and turning he observed his wife as she set about this daily ritual and offered a silent prayer that the oil would achieve the objective. Their first born, Colm, bellowed his existence from the adjacent bedroom; if the parents were somewhat lethargic he was not and his crying reminded Cait and Sean that he wanted his breakfast.

Descending to the kitchen, they heard the ringing of Ringsend Church bell calling the people to eight o'clock Mass; it was Sunday, 27th September 1931. Turning to her husband, Cait said that she would not be answering the call, for once they would have to start without her.

When her contractions started in the afternoon, Sean set off to fetch the midwife, a local woman who had delivered many of Cait's nieces and nephews. Arriving at the home, upon examining the expectant mother she advised that Sean should prepare plenty of warm water as quickly as possible. The baby, she said, would not wait too long.

Upstairs Cait set about achieving that which the Catholic Church ordained as being the most important part of her marriage, the production of another Catholic child. She strained and pushed as and when the midwife instructed. Every fibre of her body ached, she pondered that the sowing of the seed was preferable to reaping the product of their thrusting nine months earlier. Of one thing she was very certain, did Sean want any more children then he and not she should have them.

"Come on, Cait," urged the midwife, "I can see the baby's head, push harder, my love, it's almost over." Cait strained as never before, the midwife crooned her soft encouraging words, "Push, push, yes, that's it, one more time – it's all over, Cait, it's a little boy." With deft fingers she cut and tied the cord which had nurtured me through the months since conception.

The midwife lifted me so that my exhausted mother could see her second son, then placed me in warm water and washed me all over before wrapping me in swaddling clothes and placing me in my mother's arms. Having been summoned by the midwife, Sean entered the bedroom, bent over the bed, kissed and thanked mother for the gift which they agreed should be named Donal Liam. They pondered what lay ahead for the mite and, holding hands, prayed that God should bless and protect him always.

I had arrived; although I was baptised Donal Liam, I got to wondering if my name was not "Ahjasus Hesadote", such was the frequent mouthing of those who put their heads into my pram for the customary examination.

Mother said that I cried for the first ten months of my life and told the story of how, driven to distraction one day by the incessant crying, she pushed my pram to the extreme end of the garden. Within a short time a neighbour came around to enquire if mother knew that the baby was crying. "Yes," replied mother, "I know only too well that he is crying. Why do you think I put the pram to the end of the garden?"

Where do I begin? Should I commence with the old music hall joke, "I was born at an early age" or should I simply write down that detail which I recall from my early childhood and, in doing so, try not to shade over those parts which perhaps would be better left untold.

As I would be honest in my appraisal of others I hope that I am equally as honest about myself and tell it with my warts as well as my beauty spots. It is relatively easy to put pen to paper and spill the beans about others; however, it is a horse of a different colour when the person under the spotlight is yourself. As someone more erudite has said, "Oh to see ourselves as others see us". Sadly many do not recognise the crusty face in the mirror as being their own reflection – that could not be he, or she, no never, they are far more presentable than that. Yes, our own impression of ourselves rarely matches the images which face us.

Similarly our thoughts about ourselves in terms of how we relate to others, how we treat others and generally stack up in life can be poles apart from another's assessment. The person whose self-assessment aligns exactly with that of a third party has yet to be born.

I was born into what would be termed at that time as a middle class family. My parents owned the house or, if not owned, there was an intention to purchase by way of mortgage. The house, in Derrynane Gardens, Bath Avenue. Sandymount Dublin, was typical of the time, a classic three-bedroom semi-detached with a larger than average garden. Built in 1930, Derrynane Gardens and a similar set-out at the opposite side of Bath Avenue, O'Connell Gardens, were named to the memory of Daniel O'Connell, Irish politician and nationalist who successfully fought to repeal the law which barred Roman Catholics from sitting in Parliament.

Daniel O'Connell was born at a place named Derrynane in the southwest of Ireland in 1775. His fight for the repeal of the unjust law of the day was to cost him his extensive Law practice together with his estate and, subsequently, his health. His home at Derrynane was renowned for its hospitality, as we have always kept an open door, and I suppose by way of maintaining my links with dear old Ireland, my home in England has always been named Derrynane. I trust that I have never insulted this good name.

Home was very much an open door and the house was always full of people, or so it seemed. Both my parents had a large circle of friends who were always dropping in for the inevitable cup of tea and, of course, a cigarette. Looking back it seems to me that there were endless parties, when the house would be full of people singing, dancing and drinking.

My mother was an accomplished pianist who kept herself abreast with the ever-changing music scene and therefore was always able to rattle off whatever tune was setting people's feet tapping. Those were the days when everyone had a party piece and were more than willing to stand by the piano and give of their best. As I recall, some were good and some, well, they thought that they were good; as they say, God loves a trier and how some of them tried me, and kept me awake.

My mother kept a very good table, there was always a cooked breakfast and at lunchtime another cooked meal. The evening meal usually consisted of a bowl of soup and sandwiches, except for Thursdays when my father would arrive home with the makings of a gradely mixed grill. As children we naturally looked forward to Thursday nights.

My earliest recollections are associated with events which centred around a friend of my father's who was training for the priesthood, one Jack Thompson. Jack and my father grew up together in Belfast and upon leaving school both became telegram boys with the Post Office. When Jack got the calling to serve the Lord, my father moved south of the border where he enlisted in the newly founded army of the Irish Free State.

When my father and Jack met up again both were in Dublin, my father as a married man residing in Sandymount and Jack in training at Blackrock College. They were about four miles apart and, as and when time permitted, inseparable.

I remember as if it were yesterday the day of Jack's ordination into the priesthood in 1934, when I was approaching my third birthday. Myself and my brother Colm were looked after at home whilst the adults went off to this most important of ceremonies. Whilst I don't recall much of the detail when all returned to Derrynane for Jack's ordination breakfast, I do recall him signing his first Mass cards and blessing the various visitors who were present, and myself pulling at his coat for attention.

It was a day to remember and, looking at photographs of the occasion, it all comes flooding back. The next marker in my early life was Jack's departure to Africa as a missionary for the Holy Ghost Fathers, this perhaps in 1935. Everyone gathered at our house to say their farewells, then the nearest and dearest accompanied him to the North Wall where he took the night boat to Liverpool on the first leg of his journey.

The rest of the party went down to the South side of the Liffey at Ringsend where fires were lit on a slipway to coincide with the passing of the ferry boat. There was much shouting and waving as the ferry went by and I suspect a few wet eyes from the ladies who were present.

Later all gathered at Derrynane, where there would have been further weeping and, inevitably, a drop of the hard stuff. Jack was held in high regard and as can be seen from some photographs of the day he was not averse to joining in the fun which was part of the joy that was my childhood in Derrynane. The war was to prevent Jack's return from Africa until one evening in 1946 when, out of the blue, he walked in the door at Derrynane Gardens.

Lakelands Convent, where I was enrolled in 1935, had been the early seat of learning for the Maguires of Irishtown; my mother's family were part of the fabric. So it was that I must follow the long-established tradition and bow and scrape to the Holy Nuns.

Now before I go any further I must introduce another of my father's friends, Rory. Now here was a man who possessed every imaginable gift that one could wish for. He was witty and clever and above all a marvellous story teller who could keep everyone hanging on his every word. Not surprisingly he was an actor who played the then fashionable theatres of Dublin and he was constantly in demand to relate the latest gossip about back stage affairs, which he would embellish as suited the occasion.

Now, as stated earlier, Derrynane was always full of people. Rory lived with us until his marriage so, with all his associates and the usual family gatherings, things were pretty hectic for a young lad. Rory had a special party piece which involved me and was demonstrated at every opportunity when it was guaranteed to amuse, or, as in my parent's opinion, shock the assembled audience.

As we all know, this often to our embarrassment, children have the ability to latch onto words which are considered unacceptable, this even when they don't understand the meaning of the word in terms of it being good or bad. They somehow sense that we don't want them to use the word and so file it away in their sponge-like memories to be available for recall at our most inconvenient moment.

Occasionally such words register with a child more easily than Mummy and Daddy, Rory was well aware of this childlike phenomenon and eagerly set about his task in secrecy. He was a tireless and patient tutor and I a very willing student; he enunciated each of the chosen words very slowly and asked that I repeat them as loudly as my young voice would allow. "Come on, Donal," he would encourage me, "you can do better than that."

From day one Rory had impressed upon me that these tutorials were very much a private affair, this was our secret and I must not tell Mummy and Daddy about them. He told me that when I could repeat all the words clearly I could surprise my parents who would think me a big boy; as all little boys want to be big boys, particularly in their parents' eyes, I was eager to learn.

Rory named this six-word monologue "The Devil's Litany" and on cue from him I rushed forth and in a loud clear voice sang out "Pee piddle piss, pump fart shit." My party piece was a huge success; those present, knowing that Rory had tutored me, considered that he had done a grand job of work. However, in the era when children were expected to be seen and not heard some of those present did not appreciate the efforts of a budding blue comedian.

Needless to say my parents were not impressed and clipped my ear to show their disapproval. Rory of course got all the blame and, as you can imagine, I was kept out of the way whenever the house was full of people. However, he usually managed to smuggle me into the room when on cue I would go into my routine which by that time had been fine-tuned to perfection.

Back to my reign at Lakelands Convent where I received instruction for my first Holy Communion from the Nuns, in particular I recall a very nice Nun called Sister Raphael. Although she was very nice, she was strict in the sense that she would allow no talking in class.

One day I had taken a set of cigarette cards to school; I suppose I had better explain what these were. Well, at that time cigarette smoking was fashionable and to ensure continued sales and, I suspect, to encourage new smokers, and even increased smoking, cigarette cards were placed in every packet of cigarettes, one in a packet of ten and two in the twenty packet.

The topic of each card was part of a set of fifty-two themes which ranged from butterflies to boats and in our desire to complete the required set sons encouraged fathers and mothers to double their efforts and smoke more. As with similar sales promotions today, there was always an elusive numbered card which seemed to be unobtainable. Everyone, for example, had swops for number 9. Number 24, however, was a different kettle of fish; no matter how much your father smoked the elusive number 24 remained elusive, it was as if it had never been issued.

In my rush to show off my complete set of whatever it was that I had, I forgot where I was and was talking loud and clear. Sister Raphael descended upon me and taking the cigarette cards announced that she would give them to the Black Babies. This was the big punishment in Ireland in those days guaranteed to make strong children quake at the knees. ''Oh no, not the Black Babies'' was a usual cry. Sister Raphael's actions were the spur which unleashed all Rory's heinous words: ''You bloody bitch'' screamed my young voice.

Well, in Catholic Ireland, and, in particular in a convent, you don't use swear words, and most definitely not to a Nun. I feel sure that the poor Nun nigh on passed away, the class room was hushed, spellbound, riveted as it were to their seats. After what seemed like hours Sister Raphael came across and taking me by the ear marched me off to the principal, Sister Agnes. The man on his walk to the gallows felt no worse than I, he at least knew what was ahead of him; poor little me, striving to stop wetting my pants, knew not what lay ahead.

In my head on that long walk I had visions of a second Calvary at least, rusty nails being driven through my trembling flesh as the Nuns held my writhing body to the wooden cross. Was a set of stupid cigarette cards worth a death such as that? My mother had repeatedly warned me about swearing – now I would see, but too late.

Sister Raphael left me alone outside the principal's office where I was rooted to the spot. Eventually the door opened and I was taken in front of Sister Agnes, a small, round and fearful woman. She was very calm and simply said, "We have sent for your mother"; that was it, no rusty nails, at least not immediately.

It was raining cats and dogs, I was taken into the quadrangle and made to stand under a large tree to be isolated as it were from the other children, just in case I contaminated them. There I remained for perhaps an hour until mother arrived and during that time the various Sisters were to be seen pointing at me from the classrooms. No doubt whatsoever, the Black Baby threats were out, they had paled into insignificance, the biggie now was "To be treated like Donal McKenna".

When she arrived my mother went directly to Sister Agnes who was well known, and possibly loved, by many Maguires. She knew us all, and all about us. Through the years there had no doubt been some bad Maguires who had left her questioning her vocation; never, however, had the worst of the family ever gone so low as to call a Holy Nun a bloody bitch. Did Sister Agnes have the power she would have locked me up in some dark dungeon and left me there to rot; never had any of her staff been so insulted. Luckily for me she could not action her thoughts; she did, however, have the power to expel me and this she did and felt no guilt that I was not yet five years of age.

By the time that we arrived at our home I was black, blue and dizzy, the expected rusty nails would have been easy by comparison, the only words that rang in my swollen ears were "What will everyone think? What school will continue your education after disgracing yourself like that? Generations of my family have attended that convent with never a bad report, here you are not there for a full year and expelled. Just wait until your father has finished with you." In my mind I wondered why the concern for further education, when father had finished with me there would be nothing to educate.

The punishment lasted a long time. Silently I think Rory was proud of me, certainly it was he and he alone who consoled me and offered any kind words. I suppose he had also come in for some criticism because, were it not for him, the family could still walk tall in Sandymount. *He* had trained this little heathen to utter such demonic and blasphemous words. "How many times have we told you?" my parents asked Rory time and time again. "It's all very well to laugh at the little devil but laughing surely encourages him to continue; you really must work with us in our endeavours to put a stop once and for all time to his swearing.

Eventually I was accepted for further schooling at St. Mary's Star of the Sea, but long before I arrived my reputation was well known and talked about. Had I two heads I would not have attracted as much attention: "That's him that was kicked out of Lakelands Convent for swearing at a Nun!" I was something of a star attraction and pointed out to one and all, the teachers waited for me to step out of line, no Nuns here, just hard disciplinarians, some of whom took a delight in beating any youngster fool enough to break any of the many school rules.

Rule number one came into effect at five to nine each morning when the Headteacher blew his whistle; there was immediate silence in the playground, the only noise was that of running feet as children rushed to get into their correct class line in front of the Headteacher. The top class assembled in a line to his right, then the next highest class and so on across the school yard. When everyone was assembled the Head again blew his whistle when the top class marched off to their classroom, the other lines of pupils followed in like manner, there was no talking.

However, I had learned my lesson the hard way and, apart from a run in with one teacher, my time at St. Mary's was uneventful. I applied myself to all lessons and would, I think, have been something of a surprise to them in that I was usually the first with answers. St. Mary's was a hard but good school and, given that you applied yourself, the teaching was good and efficient.

Nearing the end of my days at St. Mary's, the war had commenced and with rationing forecast my parents had set about building up a store of non-perishable food stuffs, also a large stock of coal which, of course, was imported from England and would be the first item to be lost. My father managed to acquire about ten large cellophane bags of broken cocoa shells which could be used to make a very pleasant hot drink, or so it was said. When times were very bad in terms of the supply of tea, father turned to the broken cocoa but quickly turned away. When the war ended and the supply of tea eased, there were still perhaps nine bags of that stuff left.

The war years were very hard, because there was no coal other than a much reduced supply for the gas and electricity industry, and both of these most essential of services were rationed; the cooking of food was a great problem. Whereas the powers that be could control the supply of electricity by the simple expedient of pulling a switch at the appointed hour, the control of gas was rather less manageable.

Gas was only available for perhaps two hours each morning and evening to coincide with the usual start and finish times of most work places. At the designated hour, the pumps, which forced the gas along the miles of pipes required to feed the houses of Dublin, would be turned off. And that, it was thought, was it; no gas in any home until the pumps were started up again.

The Gas Authority, limited as they were in the amount of coal available to them from England, had no alternative but to ration their product; this I suspect in the full knowledge that, although they could stop the pumps at the given hour, they could not drain the gas from the many miles of piping around the city. Given this situation they immediately set about creating a new Department which would have the responsibility to ensure that people did not attempt to operate any gas appliance during the period that the gas pumps were shut down; to assist them in this regard they had a team of Glimmer Men.

Although the gas had been turned off and in spite of the danger, people continued to extract the residue from the pipes – no real pressure, just a glimmer which might warm sufficient water for a wash. It would at least preheat the pot or whatever, such that when pressure did return, the time taken to achieve boiling would be reduced. Now this was a very selfish practice and, as every household in Dublin was selfish, the end result was that when the pumps were restarted the first hour of running was needed to build up the line pressure which the use of the glimmer had reduced. In certain outlying areas the normal line pressure had not been achieved before the pumps were again stopped.

"Quick, the Glimmer Man is coming!" At such a cry a bucket of cold water was thrown over the gas cooker to cool it down, and many the false call there was. Still, it was better to err on the side of caution than to have your gas cut off, and that was the penalty should you be caught using the glimmer. The give-away was a hot cooker, hence the bucket of water by the stove.

Central heating as evident in homes today had yet to arrive; most houses were heated by coal fires and in many homes bedrooms had small fire grates. As far as our home was concerned, the main fire, situated in the parlour, provided hot water and in addition, it had an oven.

The supply of coal for domestic purposes was stopped and people had to use either wood or peat. This was an acceptable alternative in many homes. However, in others, and indeed in our main fire, which had been designed solely as a coal burner, it was very difficult to burn efficiently, if at all.

In particular peat was a problem, because of its high moisture content and the resulting up-draught that was required for efficient combustion. Air circulation was essential if any semblance of a fire was to be maintained and the end result of this was that, whereas your front might be warm, your back would be

9

freezing. The biggest problem as I recall was smoke; the room was seldom free of peat smoke and, should anyone close the parlour door sharpish-like, a partial vacuum was created in the room which then sucked whatever smoke that had been going up the chimney back into the room.

The lack of coal turned industry on its head. It certainly set it back a century in terms of efficiency; neither peat nor wood had the calorific value of coal and, as most industry used steam to drive machinery, many factories simply went to the wall. Those who survived were producing at a far lower production rate than would have been acceptable prewar and then all manner of manufacturing changes had to be designed and implemented to achieve this lower rate.

As stated, the moisture content of peat was naturally high and particularly so when the peat was not stacked and allowed to air at the bog after cutting. Because everyone now wanted peat, the interval of time between cutting and selling, hitherto at least three dry months, was reduced to weeks. The result was that upon arrival at the many "Turf Banks" which had sprung up along the canals, the peat was wet. Peat was sold by weight and not the sod; it was a seller's market and unscrupulous retailers were known to turn a hosepipe on the peat to enhance their profits.

Our nearest Turf Bank was Andrew's on the Grand Canal and a wit of the day said that, rather than issue standard water bottles to troops in the Desert, each soldier was given a sod of their turf. The reason for this was, of course, that a sod of their turf held more water than a standard water bottle. On occasion this was certainly true; you could wring the water from a sod when there had been little or no rain, suggesting that old Andrew was not averse to using the hosepipe on his stock of peat.

Properly cooked food was a problem and many a meal which was put on the table was nigh on raw. As I said earlier, necessity is the mother of invention and so many families built a sawdust fire in the garden which contraption was used to produce griddle bread. I must apologise for using the term bread, a burnt dough would be a far better term to describe this material. Eaten hot, however, it was passable.

Our sawdust fire was a standard seven-pound biscuit tin, into the bottom of which a two inch hole had been cut. The rolling pin was stuck in this hole from the inside and held vertical whilst the tin was packed tight with sawdust. It was essential that this packing was thorough and efficient, if it were not, the sawdust would collapse when the rolling pin was removed.

With the rolling pin removed the biscuit tin was mounted on some fire bricks or similar, so that a well, with an open front, was created beneath the tin. Wads of old paper were then inserted into the well and ignited, the flames would be drawn up through the centre of the sawdust in the hole from which the rolling pin had earlier been extracted.

Given a fair breeze the sawdust would quickly commence smouldering and generate heat sufficient to bake the doughy substance which had been placed on a metal plate a couple of inches above the smouldering sawdust. The process usually took a few hours, depending on the quality of the sawdust, and as said earlier, only the brave and hungry relished the end-product.

Everything was rationed and could only be obtained if you had money and the necessary coupons as issued in each individual's ration book. The coupons were more valued than money for without them you had no butter, tea or sugar or other essentials of life. Lose a pound note and usually you could borrow one until your next pay day; lose your ration book and you nigh on starved.

The Minister for Supplies, the man responsible for tea rationing, was revered in song:

"Bless 'em all, bless 'em all.
The long and the short and the tall.
Bless De Valera for our liberty, and
Bless Sean Lemass for our half ounce of tea."

Nothing is longed for more than the unobtainable. The blackmarket was one source and, even at a £1 a pound, it was selling as fast as it arrived to hand. When you consider that a tradesman would only be earning £2.50 for a forty-eight hour week you can imagine the value placed on a cup of good tea. In today's terms, with the higher level of pay and the reduced working week, it would perhaps equate to £180 per pound.

Another wartime problem was the absence of oil and petrol on the open market. Indeed, if memory serves me right, the ordinary man in the street had access to neither. What cars there were had been converted to run on gas, which was stored in a large inflatable bag set in a framework erected on the car roof, and what a sight that was. This bag was roughly four feet square by three deep and turned a car into a monstrosity.

As children we played games in the street without the worry of speeding cars or motorcycles, apart from the delivery men's horsedrawn carts every morning, the streets were free of all traffic. There were seventy-seven houses in Derrynane Gardens and I think that only two people owned cars; during the war these disappeared, so mother never worried that we might be involved in a car accident. The bicycle reigned supreme and the City centre at rush hour had to be seen to be believed: it was an amazing sight, road intersections were manned by white-gloved points duty Policemen, some of whom were more feared than the Devil himself.

Although the Premier of the day, De Valera, had declared Ireland's neutrality there was a concern that we might be forced to think differently. Lest the situation change it was essential that we were in a state of readiness and so we were prepared for some minor eventualities; we were issued with gas masks and every tenth householder was supplied with and put in sole charge and responsible for, a five-gallon water bucket together with a "stirrup pump".

It was deemed a "stirrup pump" simply because its bottom end was shaped like a stirrup and was secured to the ground by the foot of the user. It was similar to a double-handled bicycle pump and had the ability to direct a jet of water of doubtful pressure over a very short distance. Still it was better than nothing and was, I feel sure, a great asset when a few bombs were dropped on the North Strand area of the city.

Early on in the war these appliances were inspected by the A.R.P. at regular intervals to ensure that they were being maintained in good working order and readily available to combat whatever it was they were intended to combat. However, as with all good intentions, the inspection procedure was soon forgotten, this perhaps due in some measure to the fact that the person responsible for the appliances was not at home when the item had been required for inspection.

What the outcome would have been had the planned-for emergency arisen I hesitate to guess; let's suppose that the person in charge of this all important piece of fire fighting equipment was at Mass, had gone for a couple of jars or whatever, what would the outcome have been? Still, I suppose we could have trotted off to the next closest "stirrup pump" holder and requested the loan of his appliance, always of course providing that the kids weren't playing with it.

Not to be outdone in these preparations for war, the medical people together with the St. John's Ambulance Brigade and other similar well-intentioned organisations decided that they should acquaint the populace, in as far as this was possible, with a mock stage-managed war situation.

The streets would be strewn with injured people, every imaginable type of injury would be available to test the medics' reaction to stressful situations. This would be a full alert and was to be treated as a real life and death happening, it was to be impressed upon the "injured" that they should act out their part as this in turn would impress upon the medics the urgency of the condition: death was close, play at dying.

Children would act as the injured and were selected from the local schools and briefed as to the importance of their role; nothing was left to chance. Come the emergency, this would be indicated by the wailing of a siren, the lucky chosen ones were to lie down in the road adjacent to their home, strictly at a point which had been advised to them, and await the arrival of the Rescue Service who would attach a luggage label indicating the suspected level of injury to the coat to each person.

The night of this mock emergency, late November, turned out to be extremely cold and frosty; luckily it was a dry night and, as we had been promised a reward for our efforts in assisting Ireland's war preparations, we were more than willing to go along with this adult "game".

Yes, child like, we did view events as a game, children seldom if ever see danger, so it was that I lay my body down in Derrynane Gardens and awaited my rescue thinking only of what my reward would be. Hot Bovril and biscuits we had been told, we all agreed that such was a very reasonable reward and eagerly waited to be located and ferried to the local Hockey Club which building was to be commandeered as a field hospital.

I was duly located and identified as having suffered two broken legs, I lay on the road examining the stars thinking all the while of that hot Bovril and, hopefully, chocolate biscuits. When a stretcher party came within my line of vision I started to act out my injuries. "Over here, mister, please come quick, the pain is killing me." Onto the stretcher I was bundled and off in an Army lorry to the Hockey Club where I was placed on the floor with the other injured children to await the attention of a doctor.

We had lain on the floor for perhaps half an hour when an officer, probably the organiser, called for our attention:

"Bad news, chaps," he stated, "the supply wagon has been bombed and therefore the promised Bovril and biscuits are not available." All hell broke out, the injured were off that floor screaming all manner of insults to each and every adult within ear-shot and order was only restored when we were ushered off the premises.

We had been well and truly conned and the lads were of one mind, sod the war effort; in future if the adults wanted to play games they could count us out. The message must have struck home because we were never asked to participate in any other war preparation games.

Chapter Two

Primary schooling completed, I was enrolled at Westland Row Christian Brothers' School for my secondary education. Christian Brothers, like Priests, are men of the cloth who have dedicated their lives to Christ. However, unlike Priests, they renew their vows after a set period of time and continue to do so throughout their lives; a Priest gives his vow but once, and this for life.

At that time Christian Brothers had a reputation for being hard and I must say that I witnessed some punishment being given to lads which, if given today, would land the perpetrator in prison. One particular Brother was not content to thrash you with his leather; his main and favoured weapon was a length of one-inch-round pole which he would use on every part of your body, a real pervert.

Luckily they were not all like him. Most were very good and gave of their very best and, given that you worked at your lessons and completed your daily homework, you had nothing to fear.

Because of the food problems which the war had brought about, a system was introduced into schools whereby children would be given a sandwich and half a pint of milk daily, issued and eaten at going-home time. The thinking behind all this was that, at the very least, children would have an evening meal. The sandwich varied daily – jam today and cheese tomorrow – and although there was never any butter on the bread to a starving youngster that was not important.

The catch to this bounteous feast was that it was only available to those children whose fathers were dead or unemployed.

In every classroom at Westland Row there was a grained varnished cupboard on the wall wherein the teacher kept, among other things, his all important punishment piece, the leather strap. Although all leathers looked alike, standard issue as it were, the sting of each was different. Whether this was due to the differing methods of application, or as rumour had it, due to the coins which some teachers had inserted between the two sections of leather which made up the strap, I don't really know. What I am certain of is that, whereas one teacher could numb your entire hand with one strike of his leather, another could not achieve the same result with six of the best.

Now back to the cupboards; when in a classroom early one morning before the arrival of the teacher, I inserted an old key which I had found somewhere into the cupboard lock and, to my utter surprise, the door swung open. There were perhaps six present who had seen what I had achieved, two in particular I remember, twins from South Lotts Road. I shut the door and was prepared to leave it at that until someone said, "Take the leather, Donal." Well, what was I to do? So the leather was secreted in my school bag and, as the teacher was coming, we all quickly took our places.

Although the teacher used the cupboard he had no need of his leather, therefore it was not missed during our lesson with him. On our way home that evening and when crossing the Grand Canal a ceremony was held and, to great cheering, I dropped the weighted strap into the canal. I was the hero of the day, I was everyone's champion: "Try another cupboard tomorrow, Donal, get this teacher's strap – and don't forget him, and him, and him." I was on a high – "I will rid the school of leathers, just you wait and see."

I could not get to school quick enough the next day to try another cupboard. Bingo, it worked again. Either my key was some type of master, or all the locks were the same. Whichever it was, I had access to all the cupboards and all the straps were at my mercy. In all I disposed of perhaps six straps and enjoyed every minute of it; suddenly I was everyone's best mate. At the last disposal there were dozens on the canal bridge to cheer as I ceremoniously let the strap descend into the murky depths of the canal.

My glory was short-lived. I was betrayed and next morning my eagerness to arrive early and do my dirty deed was expected. "Good morning, McKenna." This from the waiting teacher, who greeted me as soon as I entered school. "The Head would like a word with you; this way, please."

Brother Ryan (I think that was his name), quite a reasonable man, was not very pleased when I arrived. Naturally I denied it all but this was pointless because he left me in no doubt that he was fully informed of my exploits. I was doomed.

Visions of events which followed my expulsion from Lakelands Convent flashed before my eyes, the physical punishment, although quite severe, had in reality been the easiest part. The soundness of a beating lasts for a short time, this in some measure due to the fact that as a general rule the parent regrets their action within a very short time and, as we all know, we reach out, pull the wayward child to our bosom, give them a cuddle and all is forgotten.

When the parent keeps the ball bouncing day after day then you know that you have really offended them; it was not simply a question of me and my parents, it was the good name of the family which I had dragged into the gutter. The Maguires of Irishtown were a closely knit family unit, my expulsion from the convent affected them all. My good conduct at St. Mary's may have elevated me slightly in the family: "He's a little horror rankings", they may have smiled and possibly even patted my head on occasion; however, make no mistake, the rawness was still there and it was doubtful that a second helping of a family member being expelled from a school would be taken lightly.

On the way to the Headteacher's office I reasoned that I had but one option, this was to run away before news of my actions reached the family; perhaps I could stow away aboard one of the schooners which were often to be seen in Grand Canal Basin? Perhaps the Brothers would beat me to a pulp and drop me into the murky depths of the canal; once again I experienced that bladder evacuation feeling, my knees rattled like a pair of castanets.

Very softly Brother Ryan said, "Hold your hand out, McKenna", whereupon he proceeded to give me six of the best on each hand. He knew how to use a leather, years of practice no doubt, and my hands felt double their normal size when he finished. At regular intervals throughout the next few days I attended each teacher whose strap I had sent to a watery grave and was given the same punishment. Looking back, I suppose that, having tasted most of the straps in Westland Row, I can speak with some authority on the quality of each, and the methods of application of many of the teachers of my day.

Westland Row school adjoined the church of St. Andrews, beneath which there were extensive burial vaults into which most unsuspecting "new boys" were lured on the pretext of seeing something of great scholastic interest. Now, by the time the bait had been swallowed, and the lamb was on his way to what was in effect his initiation ceremony, other willing hands were in position to witness the fun, some fun.

As stated the vaults were extensive and well lit, with the light switch positioned by the entrance gates. The suspect was led forward through the newest section, then right and eventually left into the old part; this I suppose over a total distance of no more than 100 feet. As with all such places it was damp and eerie and by the time he had reached the second turning the bravest lad was feeling decidedly frightened.

Needless to say, the lad who was leading the poor lamb forward was an exceptional runner who knew his exact position relative to the exit. At a prearranged signal, when he had the suspect engrossed at a vault door, the lights were switched off and he legged it for the exit, leaving the victim alone. It is pretty well accepted that the living are a far greater problem than the dead; however, try to believe that when trapped alone in a darkened vault when you don't know which way to turn to get out.

Some screamed, some pleaded and I feel sure some wet themselves. All, without exception, were scared sick and were rooted to the spot. Eventually, upon hearing voices, you would move towards them feeling your way along the steel bars of the vaults. Depending on how much you were liked, a light would be lit at a strategic point sufficient for you to hasten forward, round the corners and see the entrance gates which you would reach at break-neck speed. Mercifully you would be alone to dry your eyes and compose yourself; after a while you would give a feeble laugh and marvel that you had survived the ordeal, and I dare say even planned your revenge on some other poor soul.

There was no school transport in those days, everybody walked to school or, in my case, jogged. School was perhaps two miles away and, as school dinners did not exist, we went home at lunchtime, a duration of one hour within which you had to trot four miles and eat a meal. Although my mother fed us well she maintained a rigid seven-day menu which meant that you never needed a calendar to establish which day it was, you simply looked at your plate and, if it was stew you immediately knew that it was Wednesday.

I hated Wednesday because trotting the two miles back to school with a belly full of stew was not easy, most uncomfortable in fact. Monday being washing day, lunch was always some concoction prepared with the leftovers from Sunday. It was simply a question of speed, as they say anything is good enough for a starving belly; there was no washing machine and mother had little time for fancy cooking – bang it in the pan, bang it on the table sort of thing.

Another hate was rain, particularly on a Monday when mother was trying to get the washing dry. That was one day when we never stepped out of line. Mother used to strip the beds on Sunday evenings and steep the bedding along with the other clothes for washing in the bath over night. Monday morning it was sleeves up and, using the scrubbing board, scrub the clothes until they were clean. Prewar, when there was limitless gas, the soiled clothes would be boiled in a large pan on the gas cooker before scrubbing.

We had a cleaning woman, Molly, who came every Wednesday to do the heavy cleaning. Molly was what we called a "Shawley" – she wore a black woollen shawl which covered her from head to waist both summer and winter. She was a lovely woman whose husband was dead and, having some young children at home, charring helped her to make ends meet.

I remember her arriving one day crying her eyes out. Mother had great difficulty consoling her until eventually she could extract the reason for all the weeping and wailing. When Molly calmed down we learned that she had been informed that morning that her young son's ship had foundered and that all hands were presumed dead. The name of the ship, the year or, indeed, any other detail is unknown to me, I do recall that Molly was never the same woman again and that she virtually gave up her work.

Molly was a great one for reading the tea cups and on many a day I rather doubt that she did any cleaning; instead her time would be spent reading the cups of people who just happened to be in the house that day. A planned chance meeting as they say.

I recall mother taking me to hospital with the intention of having me circumcised. The Doctor examined me and said that it would not be necessary, telling my mother to use Vaseline and roll my foreskin back daily. When we got home, this after calling at Potter's Chemist shop on Bath Avenue where my mother purchased a pouch-like affair, Molly was in the house.

Molly, who obviously knew where we had been, wanted to know all the details; when informed of the Doctor's prognosis she took it upon herself to do his bidding. Off I was led to the bathroom where Molly whipped off my pants and set about her work with the Vaseline. When her work in that quarter was finished, my bits and pieces were placed in the pouch which mother had bought at Potter's and this was then secured around my waist.

I said at the beginning that I would put it all down, warts as well as beauty spots.

My father was employed as an agent for a Clothing Cheque business which job took him all over the city of Dublin on his bicycle in all types of weather. When he arrived home in the evenings he would be laden down with money, usually in coin, which he had collected ruing the day. He would put all this on his desk and it was our job to sort it into piles of like coins, after which father would stack it neatly into one-pound piles. The speed with which he achieved this used to fascinate me.

18

Some evenings father would come home soaked to the skin and during the war years, when there was little or no heating, drying wet clothes was a problem which upset the entire household. I feel sure that there were times when the clothes he put on some mornings were not properly dry, but there was little else that he could do; no work no pay, so off poor father would go on his bicycle for another wetting.

My father was a very good gardener and the garden at Derrynane was the envy of many. All his spare time was spent digging and planting and examining things to make sure that the slugs were not getting established. On summer evenings, when slugs and snails were most active, myself and my elder brother would go around inspecting under plants for their telltale signs and to collect them into a tin which contained a layer of salt. We were not asked to do this job, it was expected of us and, should we not do it, we got no pocket money; again the simple rule of no work, no pay, descended even to our lowly rank.

Pocket money was two old pence per week, and with 240 to the pound it can be seen that this was less than one penny in today's terms. However, things being relative I don't suppose it was that bad; for example, you got twenty-four Mint Imperial sweets for a penny, and a two-pound loaf of bread cost threepence.

We could get into the pictures, the Regal at Ringsend on a Saturday afternoon, for tuppence, so should you decide on the pictures that was you flat broke for the week. In winter it was usually the pictures, in the good weather we would play hurling or go swimming. In my apprenticeship days I would go to the Museum or the Art Gallery.

The daily routine at home was that my brother and I took it days about to do mother's shopping in Ringsend before we set off for school. There were no home freezers in those days, not even a fridge, so everyone shopped daily, taking the order book and handing it over the counter. As each item was passed over the price was entered in the book. On Saturday mornings the book was simply handed to the grocer and left with him; on that day the order was larger than other days and had to last until Monday. On Saturday evening the grocery owner arrived with mother's order, the order book and, of course, the week's bill which had to be paid immediately.

On Christmas Eve the grocer would call on all his customers and present each with a Christmas cake and a large candle, this to show his appreciation for their continued custom. On these occasions he would be driven around from house to house by his delivery man in the horse and dray and, as he would usually imbibe at each stop, he would be legless before he returned to his shop.

The butcher's shop at Ringsend, indeed all such establishments, was far removed from the hygienically squeaky clean butcher's shop of today. The most noticeable difference was that animal carcasses were hung on a metal rail outside the shop open to the elements, including flies and suchlike but out of reach of the local dogs who on occasion were to be seen eyeing up the situation, no doubt wishing in their doggy brains that one of the meat hooks would break.

Did the butcher not have your requirement to hand within the shop, he would simply go outside with his saw and remove a suitable section from a carcass, return indoors and carve your chosen piece of meat.

I completed my secondary schooling at Westland Row and it was intended that I should continue into higher education which, at that time, had to be paid for. I don't recall that any definite plans had been made in respect of what my intentions were for the future; at that time I think the tendency was to see how you developed and take it from there.

It was perhaps just as well that plans had not been formulated for my future because Fate decided otherwise. As I have said, father's mode of transport was his faithful old bicycle. Well, one evening he was knocked off this and this simple accident was to change all our lives and put considerable stress on the family.

At the time it appeared to be straightforward. He was badly knocked about but, with no bones broken, we considered him lucky. The man who had knocked him down had taken him to Hospital, had him examined and brought him home. "He will be OK come Monday," said he as he dashed off that Friday evening and we had no reason to doubt his word.

However, come Monday morning and father's condition had deteriorated such that all thoughts of him setting out on his bicycle were forgotten. Because his salary was strictly paid on a commission basis he was very concerned with this turn of events. Mother pointed out that, whereas he might manage to depart the house, his condition was such that he would collapse shortly thereafter with the result that he would negate any benefit which had been gained from the weekend's rest. Having been assured that another couple of days' rest would bring about a full and lasting recovery he agreed to remain in bed.

Those couple of days dragged on and on, the weeks came and went and still father remained in bed; there was no money coming into the home and, had it not been for limited savings and the support of mother's siblings, we might have gone hungry. The previously harboured belief that father was on his way to a full recovery began to fade and black thoughts that he would never again set off on his bicycle became a distinct possibility. The family finances had to be given some urgent consideration.

My elder brother, having left school, was hoping for an apprenticeship at the Ringsend Dockyard. This, however, would not pay sufficient to make any appreciable difference to the family finances, so it was decided to forget about the Dockyard. Instead, what savings father possessed were invested in a small grocery shop in the Thomas Street area of Dublin.

Discussion had taken place with father's employers, who were agreeable that for a trial period of time mother could undertake the cash collecting part of his job. Any new business that developed in father's area would be dealt with by one of the other agents. My part in all this was to assist mother during school holidays and occasionally at evenings.

Although mother did her best, this was not enough to satisfy father's boss. In truth I don't think he wanted a woman on his staff, a married woman's place was in the home, not out doing men's work. As my education was something of a drain on our limited finances, it was decided that I should apply to the Dockyard for an apprenticeship, albeit such a position could reduce the coffers by a further £25.

Chapter Three

So it was that I entered the Ringsend Dockyard at the tender age of fourteen, a boy in a man's world, and a very small boy at that. An apprenticeship cost £25 and, as the wages during your first year were nine shillings and tenpence for a forty-eight-hour week, your parents effectively paid your first year's wages.

These were what some would have us believe were the good old days, I know differently, they were the Hire and Fire days where the saying was:

"Finish the job, be sure to do your very best,
And then go up the road the same as the rest."

The Dockyard carried no passengers; there was, however, a skeleton crew of regulars, and, a great many apprentices. If there was work you were called in and when the job was finished you were laid off. The Dockyard was primarily a ship repair yard and much of the work was on what was termed live ships, that is to say ships that were either loading or unloading cargo. In these circumstances, whatever work there was had to be completed to coincide with the ship's planned sailing time, or before. Everything was job and finish: finish the job and go up the road until you were wanted again.

Inside the yard, where ships were dry-docked, large gangs of men would be started for a particular job and, as soon as that was completed, they would be discharged. At holiday periods, and regardless of whether the job was completed or not, the workers would all be discharged two days before the holiday to ensure that they did not qualify for holiday pay.

Shipwrights would be taken on for dry-docking a ship at a set rate of seven shillings and sixpence (thirty-seven pence) and for this they would have to place the blocks upon which the ship would sit in whatever position the hull design dictated. They would also sort out and position the props that were necessary to keep the ship vertical on the blocks when the water was pumped from the dock – this the day before the ship arrived.

When the ship arrived in the dock and the gates were sealed, it would be centred to plumb lines which were positioned across the dock in such a way that the plumb indicated the centre point of the blocks that she was to sit on. When this position was achieved, and when the necessary props were floating in the dock with one end against the ship's hull and the other end towards the dock side, the docking Supervisor would give the order for pumping to commence.

Once the ship had settled on the blocks, the props, which maintained the ship vertical, were wedged into position and secured. This work completed, those shipwrights that were required for repairs aboard the ship were retained, the others were dismissed.

Although that was the way of things then, it always saddened me when gangs of men were sent up the road simply because they had completed a good job and successfully got a ship back to sea on time. One particular group of workers with whom I felt an affinity were the Riveting Gangs; like all apprentices of that time I had done my share of rivet catching with many of these men, so I suppose felt more sorry for them than for others.

A Rivet Gang comprised four men in my days: a Rivet Hotter, whose job it was to heat the rivets in a coke fire which was operated by a hand-bellows; two Knockers Down, a righthander and a lefthander – these men knocked down, or flattened, the hot rivets that were pushed from the inside of the ship's plating to the outside. The final team member was the Holder Up; he was the man who held the hot rivets in position, this with a short-shafted heavy hammer which he allowed to "bounce" on the rivet head as the Knockers Down flattened the rivet on the outside of the ship's plating.

The Hotter's fire was a portable piece of equipment and as the rivets were needed on the inside of the ship he would position his fire as close as possible to the Holder Up. Obviously there were times when he could not get close enough; in fact he could not even see this man, and it was at these times that the younger apprentices were drafted into the Rivet Gangs. At such times we would not be learning our proper trade. However, we never objected because, if the gang made good wages during the week, each man would give the Catcher Boy a shilling. If you were a first year apprentice this increased your wages by fifty percent so you will understand why we never objected.

A Rivet Gang had to knock down 300 rivets a day to make a decent wage; by hand that was very hard work. Given that the rivets were easy to insert into the holes they could achieve the 300 target. However, on occasion the holes were not clear, that is to say that the hole in the hull plate did not align with the hole in the ship's frame. On these occasions the holes would have to be drifted or reamed out before a rivet would freely enter.

Obviously on occasions such as these it was virtually impossible for a gang to make wages and understandably they would not be very pleased. It was not their fault that the holes were not clear, they had not made the plate, nor punched the offending holes, that was the Plater's responsibility.

Arguments often broke out between Platers and Riveters over hole alignment. The standard response by Riveters to Platers who said that the holes were good, was, "Yes, they are good, both are the right size. However, they are not opposite." I have seen such arguments end in fighting.

My weekly wage whilst an apprentice was as follows: first year nine shillings and ten pence (forty-nine pence), second year, thirteen shilling and four pence; third year, fifteen shillings, fourth year, twenty-four shillings and my last year thirty-five shillings (£1.75). By that time, however, the working week had been reduced to forty-four hours.

There were no washing facilities at the Dockyard nor were you supplied with any type of protective clothing. Some disillusioned person had proclaimed in large lettering on an outside wall for all to see "Slave Labour". This was still visible when I departed in 1952.

The part I enjoyed most about my five-year stint was working out on live ships along the quays. On such occasions I would dream dreams of the foreign lands that each ship I worked on had visited, the seas it had sailed upon and the storms it had survived. It was here that my love of the sea and shipping developed and towards 1949 all I could think of, and all that I really looked forward to, was the completion of my apprenticeship and my sailing away on some ship. My ideal ship was the *Irish Fir* of Irish Shipping Ltd., this perhaps because we always seemed to be working on her; from the day she docked until sailing day, we would be aboard doing various jobs.

Whenever my mind strayed to sailing away from Dublin, the ship which carried me off was always the *Irish Fir*. As my dreaming was always of tropic islands I don't know why I chose the *Fir*, which spent her time voyaging between Dublin and the Baltic. No scantily clad dusky maidens awaited me in that area of the world; still we never consider such minor detail in our dreams.

Although the *Irish Fir*, which had been built in Germany in 1920 as the *Agnetapark*, was no beauty, she was still my ideal ship and I eagerly followed her travels until she was sold out of Irish Shipping to the Dublin and Silloth S.S.

Company in 1949, when her name was changed to the *Delgany*. The change of ownership also resulted in her conversion from coal to oil burning and the revamp of her machinery space. When I did eventually sail away from Dublin it was the B. & I. Ferry and sadly not the *Irish Fir/Delgany* as I had so often dreamed.

Some years later, at mother's insistence, I agreed to sail closer to home and in this connection applied to Palgrave Murphy and was appointed to their *City of Amsterdam*. Arriving aboard at the appointed time I was shown to my cabin and, when I had unpacked, decided that I had better familiarise myself with the engine room. I had been advised that she was an oil-burning, triple-expansion vessel and beyond this sparse information I had no idea of what to expect below deck.

When boarding I had thought the ship familiar but, as there were many similar type ships afloat at that time, I pondered no further than to think that she was far removed from my last ship, which had been a modern tanker. The engine room gave me no clues either and it was only after we had sailed that I was to discover that my dream had at long last been realised. I had sailed away on the *Irish Fir*, albeit she was at that time in the ownership of Palgrave Murphy who had named her the *City of Amsterdam*.

On the home front all was not well with father's health, he never really recovered from the road accident. He did return to work for a short period. However, he simply could not cope. As I have said, he had to be mobile and his transport was his bicycle; a motor car was considered but he was not in favour of this as it was an admission that he had not recovered.

A claim for damages against the chap who had knocked him down had been filed and this was pending a Court hearing. The man concerned had not denied liability; however, he was strongly contesting the level of damages being claimed. Father by this time was having difficulty with walking and had virtually given up all thoughts of ever being fit enough to return to work, so I imagine the claim would have been quite substantial because father would only be aged forty-five at that time. If it were proved that the accident was the sole cause of his situation, then twenty years' loss of earnings would have to be costed.

The man who had caused the accident was a wealthy businessman and, like many such people, he did not like parting with his money. In fact, it would be safe to say that he was totally against paying out; it was this hatred which had enabled him to become wealthy. He employed the best legal brains who in turn engaged the best medical brains to investigate why it was that such a minor accident had resulted in such serious consequences. Was my father a malingerer? He obviously knew that the man was wealthy – was he therefore just trying to take him for all he could?

Father kept a brave face through all this and went for medical examinations as requested by the man's solicitors. This happened on several occasions and, as the walking difficulty appeared to centre on his left leg, and this having been the least damaged in the accident, many questions were asked that went back to father's childhood.

Finally the opposition found what they wanted. Father had been involved in an accident during the Civil War in Ireland when he had suffered damage to his upper left leg. This, it was stated, was the root cause of the problem and not the later accident. On the advice of his solicitor father settled out of court for a tenth of the damages that had initially been claimed. Father was a beaten man, and this, as it subsequently transpired, in more ways than one.

It was decided that what father needed was a proper holiday. The stresses of the past few years had taken their toll, a complete rest would work wonders. Father, mother and Dermot, my younger brother, went off on an extended holiday through England and Scotland for perhaps three months, visiting old friends with father even linking up with some cousins of his who, at that time, were living in the Barrow area. Colm and I stayed at home, painted the outside of Derrynane and generally got the place looking nice for their return.

Far from being recovered, father returned much worse and had a real walking difficulty. Now he needed a walking stick and, for much of the time, he also needed a steady arm to lean on. The Doctors could not explain nor understand what the problem was. All manner of medication was tried and the increasing medical costs were becoming a serious threat to the family finances. There was no free medical treatment in Ireland in those days, each visit by the Doctor had to be paid for as, indeed, did the medicine and pills which he prescribed; understandably therefore the Doctor was only called as a last resort.

The situation went from bad to worse until finally father was sent for some extensive examination which resulted in him being diagnosed as suffering from Disseminated Sclerosis. None of us had ever heard of this illness so we had no yardstick against which we could measure father's deterioration.

This was the last straw as far as father was concerned; although he did not fully understand what was happening to his body, he was not unintelligent, he knew that he was not going to get better. He had been an extremely active man –

consequently he could not come to terms with being reduced to a situation where he was totally dependent on others for the most basic of life's necessities.

Eventually he took to his bed and from that day it was all downhill. It was as if he willed himself to die, he had run his race and wanted out, he turned his face to the wall and appeared to shrink daily. He adopted the foetal position; this time, however, he awaited death not birth, until his final passing at noon on 22nd August 1949, a happy release for a brave young gentleman. It was my younger brother's tenth birthday.

Twenty years later, when visions of father's suffering were but an ever-fading memory, I was again to experience Sclerosis and the trauma which this causes the family unit.

My wife began to experience difficulties with walking when, on occasion, her left leg failed to respond to brain commands, with the result that periodically she had a face-to-face argument with the pavement. As ever in such situations, we made a joke of events, in the hope that this would ease my wife's growing concern; at such times we exhorted that she should dilute her tipple.

Eventually after a couple of years' discomfort, it was decided that medical advice should be sought. The joking was over, for clearly my wife had a problem which went beyond tiredness and suchlike.

The usual round of medical tests, these over perhaps six months, ended with my wife spending over a month in hospital when extensive testing was under-taken – lumbar puncture, brain scan, you name it and Norah suffered it in silence. One day when she was still in hospital, I received a telephone message to say that the Consultant would like to see me. In response to my "Have you discovered my wife's problem?" I received a simple "Yes."

Arriving at the hospital as instructed, I was directed to an office where the Consultant awaited me. In greeting me he asked that I be seated and imme-diately went into a routine which he had no doubt practised and fine-tuned over many years.

The results of prolonged and extensive testing had, he stated, confirmed that my wife had Multiple Sclerosis. Continuing, he said that there was no immedi-ate problem and, by way of taking my wife's mind off her problem, he sug-gested that I should encourage her to go back into the job market which she had left when we had married. Rising from his seat he extended his hand and wished me good luck for the future.

For some unknown reason I posed no questions to the Consultant. I simply listened to what he said and departed, no doubt leaving him with the impression that Multiple Sclerosis was old hat to me. How wrong he was and how naive was I.

Driving back home to collect the children, left with a neighbour, I reflected on my luck that at least Norah had been spared Disseminated Sclerosis, that dreaded and fearful disease which had taken my father to an early grave. I thanked Him above that he had seen fit not to saddle me with a second helping of Disseminated Sclerosis.

Later that afternoon, when I got to wondering what the connection between Multiple and Disseminated Sclerosis was, I decided that I should telephone our own doctor for advice. He listened attentively and eventually suggested that I should call at his house when he could explain matters in greater depth.

How was I to know that Disseminated and Multiple were one and the same thing? To say that I was shattered would be to understate my feelings; my world collapsed, I cursed that God should do this to me, I cursed everything and everybody. How I managed to drive home without killing myself, or others, I will never know. I knew but one thing, this that I did not have the strength to cope with what I was sure lay ahead.

Certainly my mother had coped but then she was a woman and she did not have two young children to consider. Suddenly all which had appeared so rosy a short while ago was gone, the warm dreams for our future life together as the complete family unit was but an imaginary thing which would never be realised.

I pondered our future long into the night and could see nothing which offered hope. My father's ending, so long forgotten, was fixed vividly in my mind's eye and nothing would clear that sight.

I cried, I dozed and cried again. I prayed that it was all but a mad dream, only to realise that this was not the case, this was for real. I prayed that God would give me the strength to surface from my turmoil, He failed me so I set about cursing Him and all His Angels and all His Saints, They were nothing but a shower who cared little or nothing for me and mine, and as such they were not worthy of my prayers.

I reached what I now know was rock bottom in the early hours of the morning. I knew but one thing and this was that I could not continue, nor could I leave the children to observe and suffer their mother's deterioration to her early death, a situation which I had observed with my father.

As a caring parent I had a responsibility to protect my children from such a situation and this I now concluded I must set about as soon as possible. The children would be put into the car and I would make for the M6 and drive at full speed into one of its many concrete bridges, a quick and painless ending to everything that now troubled me.

Although I may have deserted God, clearly He had not deserted me; yes, in spite of all my cursing He was all forgiving and at the deepest point in my life He reached out and pulled me back to reality. In doing so He indelibly etched into my mind the fact that third class living is better than first class dying. Life, no matter how difficult, is a blessing which should be cherished. Although He helped me to reconsider my thinking, so that I did not take that final fateful step which would have ended my own and our daughters' lives, my mind was in turmoil for a number of years.

Knowing my wife as he did, our own doctor suggested that I should not divulge that she had Multiple Sclerosis; this, he stated, was in the best interests of her future well being; so began an eight-year period of deceit when the only people who knew of the problem were my in-laws and close friends. Clearly my wife, an intelligent woman, had suspicions that she was not being told the truth and that the seriousness of her condition was being denied her, in particular she felt that I was more informed about her condition than I admitted.

Those were stressful years which, on the face of it, appeared not to bother me unduly, that is externally; internally, however, in particular in the subconscious, all was far from normal and matters finally boiled over in the eighth year of my deceit, the year when my wife reached the big four O.

As I had never been a big sleeper it did not concern me that suddenly my sleeping pattern deteriorated such that I became something of a walking zombie. The doctor prescribed sleeping pills, adding that I should only take them in extreme conditions and, even then, only one at a time. Eventually I reached a point where I could not attend work, my scalp was covered in pimples and, in spite of taking considerably more than the prescribed dose of sleeping pills, I could not sleep, in the final week I never ever bothered to go to bed.

Attending the doctor so that he could prescribe something for my scalp he suggested that the cause of my problem was worry; yes, I replied, I'm worried, about the pimples. He was very patient and started to question me about everything, wife, children, work, nothing serious there. He then questioned me about my parents and, when I answered that my father had died as a result of Disseminated Sclerosis in his mid-forties, the doctor asked no further questions.

The problem was my subconscious, my wife had turned forty and as my father, who had a similar condition, had died in his forties I had visions of history repeating itself. The doctor advised that the time had come when I must inform my wife of her condition; the problem, he added, concerned the whole family, they should therefore be acquainted with the full history of my wife's ailment, I must not continue the deceit.

I did as advised and that night climbed into bed for the first time in over a week, and slept; I was back at work the following week and never took another sleeping pill. From this I learned a most important lesson, as much as we may wish it to be, within marriage, we are not, and should never attempt to be, an island, the shared problem is indeed halved and this to the benefit of the entire family.

During that time I continued to fight with God, never really accepting that He could love me as much as I thought He should. On reflection, God was not the only one who suffered my anger. Try as I did, my attitude was not limited to the home and there were times when my despair and anger spilled over such that work colleagues suffered intolerably.

To those who on occasion must have suffered my anger I offer my unreserved apology, belated I know, but none the less sincere. To those who, I suspect, understood the turmoil which was my constant companion, I say God Bless you, your support through those dark, dark times was greatly appreciated, I shudder to think of the consequences had you not been supportive. On a lighter note I pray that your donkey never suffers from gout and should your mode of transport be four wheels rather than four legs, then my prayer is that your sparking plugs should never fail to brighten your cylinders.

Chapter Four

Before I proceed further I should really recount some early family holidays which were always spent with father's sister, Mary, in Belfast. Most of our summers were spent at 48 Albert Street, which used to be off the Falls Road. I say used to be simply because, from what we see on the television these past few years, I rather doubt that any of that particular part of Belfast still exists. This was pre–1939 and even in those days it was a cruel place, and very difficult for us to come to terms with.

In Dublin we had precisely the same religious mixture yet we managed to live in complete harmony. In Derrynane Gardens there were seventy-seven houses and, whilst the majority were Catholic homes where the children went to different schools, this was the only difference. We played together daily and there was never any religious intolerance whatsoever. We were all children of Ireland growing up to love being Irish, and wondering all the time why things were so different up north.

When out playing in Belfast with my cousins they would say, "We don't go down there, THEY will beat us up," and sure enough THEY would, should you be fool enough to enter. The end walls of houses proclaimed in large letters "F--- the Pope", on others "Hell Roast the Pope". As I have said, it was very hard for us to understand and upon our return to Dublin friends would never believe my account of events. Remember, there was no television to bring the reality of such happenings into your home each evening, it was mainly word of mouth, and kids were known to enlarge upon things.

When my uncle got the shutters out to board up the windows, this on July the 11th, it was mother's signal to leave Belfast and return to Dublin. July 12th was marching day when all Catholic homes were considered fair game for stones through the windows or worse. Drunken louts swaggered through the streets behind the big drums seeking out Catholic areas to vent their bitterness.

Relating such happenings to school friends later in Dublin, I feel sure that they thought that I was spinning a tale. It is incredible that in such a short distance attitudes should be so different. My father departed Belfast simply because, as a Catholic, he was a second class person, a situation that was to remain in existence until perhaps 1969 when finally, as a result of investigations by the then Home Secretary, James Callaghan, the truth was acknowledged.

As a young lad I joined the Irish Scout movement in which I was to spend several happy years. Scouting at that time, and particularly through the war years, was quite basic in that we had none of the accoutrements that are accepted as being an essential part of today's Scouting. For example, when we went hiking, every Sunday throughout summer, we *did* hike. Off we set with our bags on our backs to some predetermined destination, usually about five miles away, where we would set up camp.

The usual drill was that a party was detailed to collect firewood whilst others would prepare to cook a meal once a fire had been lit. This routine would only vary in the sense that your duties differed each week, collecting wood, preparing food, cooking, and, finally and most important, cleaning up to ensure that the area was left as we had found it.

We went further afield on Bank Holiday weekends when we would go camping into the Wicklow mountains. On these occasions we would get transport to within five miles of the intended camp and walk the remaining distance. The routine whilst there was the same as when we went hiking; additionally, we would prepare for merit badges and, if the Scout Master thought you proficient enough, you would be examined at camp.

Annual camp was usually in August and the venue was a place called Knocksink not far from Enniskerry. I spent many weeks there as a boy and enjoyed every minute of it. Indeed, after I had left the Scouts and when I was working, I returned there many times.

An Assistant Scout Master was a man called Paddy Byrne, whose full-time occupation was as a sailor on the sailing ships that plied the Irish sea at that time. I recall that he was on the *Mary B. Mitchell* when she was wrecked on the north coast of Scotland in the early forties. Luckily, Paddy, and I think all the crew, survived that tragic event.

A particular Scouting event which I recall quite clearly was a camping session for an Endurance Badge. Five of us, including my brother Colm, set off for a spot pretty well at the foot of the Sugar Loaf Mountain in Wicklow to set up camp for three weeks and to live rough, and if possible, off the land.

On that occasion we took a bus to Enniskerry and hiked the five miles or so to the selected camp site, all this in fine rain which meant that we were pretty well soaked through by the time that we arrived at our destination. Undaunted we erected the two tents and, as far as was possible under the conditions, we set about preparing the site to our best advantage.

By that time the rain had come on pretty heavily and it had turned cold, this in spite of the fact that it was August. At this point we attempted to find some dry sticks to start a fire. However, search as we did, we were not successful and finally we gave up, ate cold offerings, and went to bed.

The next day was a little better and eventually we did manage to get a fire going so we could have a hot meal. The weather, however, never really became summery and, overall, nothing turned out as anticipated; all in all, it was pretty rough, with my attempt to roast a full leg of lamb being a complete fiasco. Because we never got a really lengthy period of sunshine firewood was always a problem and, as a consequence, we could not get a proper roasting fire; the leg of lamb was charred on the outside and raw for the better part. We were hungry and in spite of much protesting it was eaten.

We stuck it out for the twenty-one days and returned home never having had a proper wash during that time. My mother said that we had never washed at all; she reckoned that my neck was as black as coal. You know how mothers go on about such things. It was only half black, and anyway I needed that dirt to keep me warm.

I had told my wife about that event and how I had fancied a properly cooked leg of lamb ever since. Can you imagine my surprise when one day she actually put a full leg of lamb in front of me and said, "Get your teeth around that." I did and, my word, did I enjoy it.

After the Scouts, when I was working, we still went off camping in our summer holidays. By that time, however, we all had bicycles and we ventured further afield, spending holidays in Avoca on several occasions and also at a place called Clara, which was at that time listed as the smallest village in Ireland. Clara was, I think, my last camp; I have visited there a few times since and it has always thrilled me to just stand and observe, dwelling awhile on my youth and enjoyment of life at that time. Alas, sweet youth, you have left me, you are gone forever. Your memory, however, will remain fresh in my mind for all time.

The other diversion of my youth was dancing. We went dancing at least once a week, this on a Saturday night to the St. John's Ambulance Hall in the City Centre. There would be perhaps twelve of us, lads and girls, and mainly from Derrynane Gardens; off we would go on the bicycles, and not always one to a bike, praying that it would not rain, or at least not too heavily if it did.

Big bands were all the rage then, Joe Loss, Harry Gold, Oscar Rabin and many others whose names escape me. All visited Dublin and were a MUST when they did. The venue for the big bands was usually either the Crystal Ballroom or the National and you can bet your bottom dollar that I was at the top of the queue to get in.

Although we were a mixed gang of lads and girls there were no relationships between the sexes. In fact, I rather doubt that we considered ourselves in those terms. We were, I suppose, eighteen or nineteen and pretty well unkissed. The only time there was any kissing was at parties when we played "spin the bottle"; we were certainly different to youngsters of today who are in and out of bed on their first date.

The Church, I suppose, was a controlling factor in that the thought of having to confess any sexual happenings to the Priest was sufficient to quell any God-fearing lad's urges. Should he reach a point where God was forgotten, he could be sure that the girl had not forgotten, and as far as any of my contemporaries ever got was a hand on a coat-covered breast and for such bravery a slapped face.

I am pretty sure that all of the gang from Derrynane Gardens were still virgins when I went off to sea in 1952. I certainly was and my ignorance of such matters was really untrue, I did not have a clue; a period as far as I was concerned was the duration of a lesson. My mother used to give me a note to go to the chemist for sanitary towels; these were always handed over in plain brown paper wrapping and, like some of my mates who, like me, had no sister to run such errands, we honestly never knew what they were, and that was at nineteen years of age. I was truly Irish, green as far as such matters were concerned.

Around that time my uncle Paddy and some of his contemporaries organised concerts locally, perhaps every three months. We all joined in and did our bit, be that singing or dancing or even acting in the sketches which made up the night's entertainment. The show, which usually lasted about three hours, ran for seven nights and was, as I recall, very good.

I was a boy soprano and really enjoyed singing. When I was perhaps about nine years of age I was enrolled at the Rita Mooney School of Acting which was at that time situated on Pearse Street. I did little acting nor, as I recall, did I receive any acting tuition, I did, however, sing my little head off and was always included in the troop that Rita selected to go out and entertain at some function or other. A favoured venue was the Seaman's Institute on Aston Quay.

I never really understood the set-up at that School, because we were regularly out giving concerts for which I feel sure Rita would have charged a fee. I got nothing save transport and a bite to eat.

When I was perhaps fifteen I did eventually do some acting, this for the annual Holy Ghost Fathers' concert at Rathmines Town Hall. A neighbour of ours, Tommy Lyons, was in the business and was responsible for arranging and directing a comedy farce each year which was the ''show stopper'' as it were of the one-off concert. This was really great fun and much enjoyed by those Tommy selected to participate, competition was keen and you had to achieve a good standard to be included in the party.

I acquired a liking for the ''Black Stuff'' at an early age so it was no surprise that, when I started work and had the price of a pint in my pocket I became a regular visitor to Paddy Gill's at the bottom of Barrack Lane in Irishtown. I chose this particular haunt because it was something of a singing house where nightly the very best were to be heard rendering the popular songs of the day, and of course the great Irish standards.

There was neither piano nor microphone, you simply stood up and let it all come out to the very best of attention; regardless of how good or bad you were, you got the best of attention. The difference showed at the end: if you got no applause then you knew that you should sing dumb in future.

Drinking was mainly a weekend event and certainly so in my case when in my early years, pocket money from my weekly wage of nine shillings and ten pence was two shillings and sixpence (twelve and a half pence). I joined in the singing but one night a week. Porter was sevenpence a pint and stout eightpence (240 pence to the pound) when I first went into Paddy Gill's, my weekly pocket money afforded me two pints and a few cigarettes. It follows therefore that, although I went drinking at fifteen years of age, my consumption by today's standards was of no consequence.

My pocket money could be increased by working overtime. My mother said from day one of my working life that such money was mine in total; it was my free time, should I have to work late then it was I and not the home that should profit. On repair work, particularly on working ships on the docks, overtime was regular and compulsory. Night school even took a back seat on occasion, as the Foreman once said to me, "Bugger school, this ship has to sail tomorrow."

There was no day release then, you went to Technical College at night and met all your expenses out of your own pocket. Each term cost seven shillings and sixpence, in my first year almost a week's wage; you were required to attend two nights a week from 7.00 to 9.00 p.m.

What with night school and overtime, I seldom had free time through the week so everything was fitted into the weekend and, boy, did we burn the candle through those two days. We extracted every last minute and lived them to the full, falling into bed late Sunday night shattered and dreading the morning.

We were a pretty close family in those days, this perhaps because family unity was considered more important than it is today, when many cease to communicate once they have married and left the nest. My aunts and uncles, on my mother's side of the family, were regular visitors to our home, as indeed we were to theirs, so we always knew of each and every family development, be this a birth, marriage, death or whatever. Family gatherings were frequent particularly at Christmas when there were set days for everything – our house on Christmas afternoon, Uncle Paddy's on Boxing Day afternoon and so on through the family.

At Christmas the big thing was the Christmas pudding. Each aunt had her own special recipe, this handed down through generations within that particular family branch and added to, or taken from, as each aunt thought best. The pudding was eaten cold, cut into little fingers and accompanied with a glass of sherry; its texture, colour and flavour was marvelled at; how long had it been boiled, how long had it been allowed to hang in its pudding cloth before it was finally uncovered and put on a plate, had the aunt fed it anything? All these were important questions and I rather doubt that the enquirer expected to get a proper answer, for to do so would of course spoil the fun.

If I recall correctly the pudding was not opened until Boxing Day when, after dinner, it was cut and pieces placed in a cast iron frying pan and fried without the addition of any oils or fats. The pudding was fried until it had a crisp outer surface, then eaten with custard. Thereafter the pudding was eaten cold.

Throughout the year the family would gather for picnics, in particular when the blackberries were ripe and ready for picking. As a general rule we met at a place called Ballanteer in County Dublin, and each family would bring a different type of food to be pooled at eating time. My mother's egg and onion sandwiches were always the first to be devoured and, to this day, an egg and onion sandwich remains my favourite.

Mother spent a lot of time in hospital when we were young children, and at such times we were taken to mother's sister Gertie who lived at Drumcondra. Gertie had four daughters, Maeve, Joan and twins, Olive and Dorothy. Because Gertie was widowed shortly after the birth of the twins, she had returned to work and engaged a Nanny to look after the girls, the house therefore was pretty well regimented. Nanny was very nice but she was strict and it never paid to step out of line. Bed was a set time, so also was getting up, neither a minute before not a minute after, it was precise.

Preciseness with Nanny – she was always called Nanny – extended to your bowel movements; that which went in daily was required to be excreted daily and your personal potty was inspected to ensure compliance with that particular rule. Regardless of how you performed through the week, Friday night was Sennapod Tea Night, when each was required to drink a cup full of the most obnoxious green-coloured liquid imaginable.

Come Saturday morning the six of us were herded into the toilet and sat on our potties, Nanny stood at the end of the toilet by the door, and exit was only possible when you had proved to her that the Sennapods had worked. The back of my neck may have been dirty on occasion when staying at Drumcondra; however, my bowels were scrupulously clean.

During the summer holidays Gertie used to rent a cottage at Shankill to which Nanny and the children were sent for the entire school holidays. Myself and my brother Colm were lodged there for at least a couple of weeks each year and for my part I always enjoyed myself, due to the fact that I had latched onto a local farmer, who took me out on his milk round in the mornings, and also let me ride the hay carts when hay ricks were being taken back to the farm. All in all, holidays at Shankill were really an enjoyable treat.

My mother had relations at Warrenpoint, although to this day I am not sure of the connection. Occasionally we spent a holiday there with one or another of this family and I recall that the elder of the family owned a number of small ferries which plied Carlingford Loch between Warrenpoint and Omeath in Southern Ireland.

At that time, and particularly during the war years, these ferries were very busy taking people across the loch, which was in effect across the border where unrationed materials were easily obtainable. The slipways where they landed were lined with stalls which offered the required items for sale and thereby relieved the purchaser of the need to go into the town. In particular cigarettes were in great demand and people on return trips were laden down with supplies. Looking back I seem to recall that cigarettes and tea were the main ''cargo'', food appearing to be less important than either of these items.

During the war things were pretty hard in Dublin, for apart from the rationing of both gas and electricity most food items were also rationed. In particular I recall that we never saw a banana from the start of the war until well after it had finished. As always, necessity is the mother of invention and some bright spark came up with the idea of making your own bananas, quite simple, and at the time quite enjoyable. Bananas were ''made'' at least once a week in our house and used as a spread on bread; the process was to boil parsnips until they were quite soft, then they were mashed. When the mashed parsnip had cooled banana essence was added and, hey presto, you had banana. Presented as a sandwich an experienced person would have difficulty in fliinding fault with the offering; the inexperienced, mainly the young, who had never known the thrill of unzipping a banana to reveal its hidden treasure, knew no better and so were satisfied that they had indeed eaten banana as part of their meal.

There was no substitute for an orange and so it was that, like the banana, many youngsters only knew of their existence through pictures. This situation remained pretty much unchanged until after the war ended, and even then, they were not always available.

I recall working on a ship in the Alexander Basin and seeing oranges being unloaded from an adjacent ship, the attention which this operation attracted said it all; Supervisors were everywhere as indeed were the Dock Police, and chance passers-by could be forgiven were they to conclude that gold ingots were being discharged. Myself and another apprentice, Tommy Kiernan from Stella Gardens, observed from afar and with saliva dripping from our chins saw the dockers being chaperoned as the cases of oranges were wheeled into the warehouse.

In all our visits along the docks we had never seen such a level of security and in spite of the obvious danger we were agreed that, at the very least, two of those oranges would be ours. Clearly we could never hope for success from our current position which was to the front of the warehouse. As the warehouses were double sided it was decided that we should go around to the opposite side in the hope that we might find an open door, or if not open, hopefully it would not be locked in which case we could perhaps slide it sufficiently for one of us to gain entry.

They say that luck favours the brave; arriving at the other side of the warehouse we discovered that there were no ships immediately opposite the required door, we also found that the door was slightly ajar. Unlike the experienced felon we stood around looking up and down the docks to check that we were not being observed until finally we made our way to the door when I, being the smallest, slipped through and made my way to the back of the stacks of cased oranges; my accomplice was to keep "Nicks" in the door-hole and signal should he see anybody approaching.

The oranges were packed in slatted crates where the distance between slats was such that the fruit would not fall out; I eagerly made my way to the nearest stack and with relative ease managed to part the slats and extract two oranges which were quickly pocketed. Easy, thought I, take another two, why stick at one apiece when the coast was clear and the fruit so handy; I turned to indicate my intentions to Tommy who it appeared was waving at me.

I had no sooner returned my attention to the orange case when I was given the full force of a size ten boot up the backside such that I was lifted off my feet. Tommy had indeed been waving; the signal, however, was not "Well done, Donal," but, "run like hell". This I did with all haste exiting the warehouse door like a scalded cat, I was halfway up the dock before my mate was aware that I had passed him. I need not have bothered, we were not chased, this I suspect because whoever it was who footed me up the "Jacksy" thought that he had detected me before I had managed to steal any fruit.

We departed the Alexander Basin, past the Dock Police and made our way to the Corporation ferry, the oranges were only removed from my pocket when we landed at Tobin's corner; stolen fruit never tasted so good.

Chapter Five

The Church played a big part in our young lives and we walked in fear of the Priest. It was as though the Priest could see our souls, and in doing so, he knew when we had sinned – it was not necessary to confess, he knew. Not true, of course, but try to convince a young lad of this when he has just made his first Holy Communion and he will not believe you.

My first Confession, prior to my first Communion, was quite an innocent affair supervised by the Nuns. The Priest, aware that this was your first such encounter, was very supportive and eased you through the event, making you feel that it was very natural to kneel before him and to relate all your misdeeds. Understandably he wanted to instil in the young the belief that Confession to God through a Priest was good for the soul. He wanted you to return week after week throughout your life, to frighten you at that early stage would be counter-productive.

Whilst I can't recall the detail of my first Confession, I do recall a subsequent Confession and the trauma endured before it was over. Mother took us to Confession every Saturday afternoon. Confession times were 3.00 to 4.00 p.m. and 7.00 to 8.00 p.m. and at that time four Priests would be hearing Confession and there was always a queue outside each Confessional. For a youngster at that time, it was quite an ordeal.

When I awoke that Saturday morning my bed was a shambles; surely I had not slept with the coarse sheets next to my bare flesh, but then had I slept at all? Had I not been paraded outside the Church in sack cloth and ashes, a sinner with my inner soul bared for friends and neighbours alike to see and point the finger of scorn: ''Always knew he was a sinner,'' I could hear them say.

But of course I had slept, and as usual I had been well tucked up between clean sheets by my mother, who had kissed my cheek and asked God to protect me, and keep me free from sin, as if a five-year-old child was capable of sin.

But I *had* sinned and this had been the reason for my troubled sleep, I knew that I must confess my sin to the Priest and through him ask for God's forgiveness. My young heart pounded within me as I relived the recent nightmare; full of shame I knelt at my bed and fervently implored that God should give me the strength and courage to go to Confession at 3.00 p.m.

As is usual in such troubled times, when some misdemeanour must be admitted, the hours flew by and at 2.45 p.m. mother had me washed and ready for Church. The walk there was a trial in itself. My heart was ready to burst, at the very least I felt that it would jump out of my mouth. I was a very frightened lad, my steps were smaller than usual and my legs felt as if they were elastic, incapable of carrying me forward, bending any which way rather than the correct way. Mother was continually reminding me to hurry, as the Church would be packed. Was I tired? she asked. "An early bed for you tonight, my lad, Holy Communion at 8.00 a.m. Mass tomorrow morning."

I felt sure that she was aware of my reason for not walking at my usual pace. My heart pounded all the harder when I considered that perhaps she, like the Priest, had the ability to see my blackened soul. I considered that the least penance he would give me would be the Stations of the Cross, these on hard peas. In my reverie I wondered who it was who put the peas under your knees as you went from one Station of the Cross to another. Perhaps there was a box of peas at the first Station which you took around with you as you went; at each Station you scooped some out and placed them under your knees as you knelt down, either that or the Priest summoned the Sexton who went around with the sinner to ensure that they did use the peas correctly.

Whatever the routine, everyone in the Church would know that I was a sinner, my mother included, and saint that she was she would not condone sin, not even in her own son.

The ringing of the Confessional bell brought me back to reality, at which point we were entering the Church door and, seeing the crowds inside, mother whispered that we would be there for an hour at least. Observing the crowds I considered them all saints: no pounding hearts there only a peaceful glow and a great love of God, all eager to enter the Confessional and open their heart to the Priest, who would listen in silence and then, as God's agent here on earth, cleanse their souls and absolve them of their sins. Oh, that I had never sinned!

Dear God, I will never sin again, honest I won't – as if "honest" was necessary, for who would tell lies to God.

Following my mother I dipped my finger in the Holy Water font and, blessing myself with the Sign of The Cross, proceeded down the aisle to a Confessional. The Church was almost in complete darkness, the only light was that which filtered through the many coloured windows which featured the various saints.

I was awed by the spectacle. Never before had I seen Christ so prominent; he hung crucified in blue, red and green behind the main altar, His bright red blood cascaded down His face, hands and feet, blood that was flowing because of sinners such as I. Were it possible, I would get up and stem the flow of blood and bathe your aching head.

My small heart was full of remorse that I was responsible for God's suffering, tears welled in my eyes and I was thankful of the darkness which left me in shadow, alone with my private grief.

The Confessionals were on either side of the Church, on the outside walls situated in the darkest positions between windows, and being so positioned they really were quite awesome. The box had three doors, full doors to right and left with a half door topped with a dark green curtain in the centre behind which the Priest sat doling out penance to sinners such as I.

I knelt beside my mother on the bare wooden kneeler, feeling nothing of the small pieces of grit which dug into my knees, my head bent in silent prayer: "Blessed Mother of God, please give me the strength to confess my sin." Sitting up in the pew I began my patient wait for my turn to enter the Confessional. As one person emerged and was replaced by another, we moved along the line.

An old lady emerged her Rosary entwined in her frail white hands, the contented look on her face said it all, she had made her peace with God, gladly confessing all through the Priest who had absolved her sins. I watched as she went to a side altar where she knelt in prayer, her fingers moving over the beads of her Rosary, Hail Mary, Holy Mary.

Eventually mother ushered me into the Confessional and shut the door behind me. I never knew that it could be so dark or so lonely. I soon knew what sweat was, I sank back on my heels holding myself to stop the pee gushing forth. Above the pounding of my heart I could hear the faint whisper of the confessor in the opposite compartment as they made their peace with God.

I recalled the Nuns' tuition prior to my First Confession; no need to worry, they had said, you are speaking to God, not to a Priest, and remember, it is good to cleanse your soul. However, at that time I had not sinned so it was not an ordeal. If this was good for me, it was beyond my comprehension, certainly I did not feel good.

Suddenly the Priest opened a small hole in the dividing partition and I could discern his face behind a grill. I came erect to my knees as the Priest said, "Yes, my son." At first I was speechless, then my sins washed over my tongue like the incoming tide over a pebble on the beach.

"Forgive me, Father, for I have sinned, it is one week since my last Confession."

The Priest's gentle voice encouraged me, "Go on, my son."

"I told lies, Father, and I gave cheek to my mother."

"What sort of lies?" enquired the Priest.

"I told my mother that I had not been caned in school when I had."

The Priest, all knowing, replied, "My son, it is always easier to tell the truth because one lie requires another to cover it up, then another is required to cover that one, and so it goes, on and on. Do you understand, my son?"

"Yes, father," I replied, "I won't tell any more lies."

"Is there anything else, my son?" enquired the Priest. He knew, he really could see into my black heart. What will he say when I tell him? Sensing my unease the Priest encouraged me to tell him all about it: "Come on, my son, don't be afraid."

If only he knew how afraid I was.

"Father, I have had evil thoughts," I blurted out. "Father, I wished that the teacher's cane would break yesterday when she was caning me."

The Priest was silent, flabbergasted I thought by the gravity of this sin from one so young. Finally he spoke. "Son, you were caned yesterday for doing wrong in the classroom, you then wished that the cane would break; then, as if that were not enough, you told your mother that you had not been caned. You see, son, it is as I have said. Because of one sin another was committed to cover it over; therefore, it is always easier to tell the truth. Now for your penance say three Hail Marys."

Mother was waiting when I came out of the Confessional. When we both went to the main altar, kneeling I promised God that I would never sin again. This same promise was repeated many times through the years and to this day I really can't understand how people can be content to continue making promises which they know they are incapable of keeping. These promises are made to God, surely He deserves better than that? You can carry on in that fashion with a friend perhaps, but with God, surely that can't be right. That He accepts such treatment must surely prove that He is indeed a very special person.

Confession in later years became something of a farce, particularly when there was something to confess. At such times we would make our way to Fr. Ryan at St. Mary's Star of the Sea, who had a hearing problem. Yes, we even cheated with Confession; we would whisper our sins, in spite of Fr. Ryan's repeated requests to ''Speak up, my son.'' Were we to speak so that he could hear us, so too would the entire Church, so we continued to whisper, happy in the knowledge that Fr. Ryan gave everybody three Hail Marys for penance. Needless to say, all the sinners were to be found outside his Confessional.

However, there were times when the Priest behind the grill was not Fr. Ryan and at such times, and when the truth of the situation was known to those waiting to confess, you could sense the fear in your neighbour on the kneeler. On such occasions the three Hail Marys became the Stations of the Cross, or perhaps a full Rosary. Whichever, such a penance would last quite awhile and would therefore be an embarrassment as others would note that you had been given more than was usual.

On such occasions I have seen people get up from the queue and leave the Church, or perhaps go to another Confessional where there were less people, so that at least they knew who they were dealing with behind the grill. Each of the Priests attached to the Church were known in terms of the severity of the penances they doled out; it was like a sliding scale where, in my time, the best was Fr. Ryan because he was deaf, and at the other end of the scale was Fr. Perkins, who was a sackcloth and ashes man.

The hardened sinners would get to Church well ahead of starting time and position themselves in prayer so that they could see the Priests emerge from the Vestry and observe which box they entered. Each Priest had his regular box with his name on a card over the door. On occasion, sickness or indeed holidays, the Priest behind the grill did not match the name over the door; when this occurred you can be sure that some sinner would be caught out. However, it was amazing how word got around when this changed situation occurred; somebody would always warn you so you could change your plan.

As I have said, we cheated. When we did get a hard penance we would only do a little of it in Church, promising God that we would say the rest at home that night. The reason? Well, it was not wise to advertise that you were a sinner who had been given the Stations of the Cross or similar, for somebody might tell your parents and then there would be trouble. So it was that we cheated.

Sad to relate but fear ruled as far as the Church was concerned. Did you not go to Mass, someone was sure to comment and ask why not. So it was that Mass was seldom if ever missed, similarly with all other Church functions: you had to be seen. Were you not seen, then you had not attended and your absence had to be explained.

At specific times through the year the Church held what were called Retreats, when real fire and brimstone Priests would attend the Church and preach each evening on a different topic. Each Retreat ran for a full week, one for men, one for women and, finally, one for the children. During the week you were expected to attend Church twice each day, Mass in the morning and then the sermon in the evening, in all you would be in Church for perhaps two hours each day.

Some of these Priests, who were I believe specially trained, could put the fear of God into the hardest of men. It was if they had the ability to see who the real sinners were. You could see them in the Pulpit pointing, and feel that they were pointing directly at you, when you would cower down in your pew thereby drawing further attention to yourself. I can say with all honesty that those Priests put many a sinner back on the straight and narrow – not for good, mind you, just temporarily.

Yes, those Priests really put the wind up people and the local publicans suffered most in that there was always a drop in sales during Retreat week, particularly men's Retreat. As I type I can hear the familiar cry – no, scream, ''The demon drink, the devil's own brew'' and I see the finger pointing and know full well that it is me that it is pointing at; honest, honest not another drop, ah go on, Father, you would not have me burn in hell, not you a Holy Priest. You would? Ah bad cess to you then.

''Bad cess to you'' – better explain that. Well, this saying is Irish and goes back to the days before the flush toilet and the Sewage Works. In those days everyone had a cess pit (septic tank), in their garden and, should it not work correctly, or have been constructed wrongly, then it would have to be dug out, not a very nice job. It follows therefore that the worst possible injury that could befall anyone was that their cess pit should cease to function correctly and require emptying or, indeed, reconstructing; so, ''Bad cess to you'' was not a very nice thing to wish anyone.

The story goes that two young lads had each had a sexual relationship which went beyond Mrs. Hand. Now, Confession was essential if they were to regain God's grace and the lads, knowing the local Priests, and the penance that such an admission would bring, decided to seek confession in some Church where they were unknown. The advice was sought of a workmate who resided in another parish. Was there, they enquired, a priest of Fr. Ryan's standing in his parish? There most certainly was, came the reply, Fr. Hogan's your man for sure.

Armed as they were with a name, and a Church, the lads set off the following Saturday, somewhat apprehensive but easier in their minds than they would have been had they been going to their own Church. Rather than follow each other into the Confession Box to admit to fornication, it was agreed that there should be an interval of some thirty minutes before the second sinner entered the box. No point in rocking the poor Priest to his foundations.

They tossed a coin to see who should go first and the loser took his place in the queue to await his turn to confess. "Bless me, Father, for I have sinned," began our lad. "It's a month since my last Confession, this due to the fact that I have been moving home and only settled hereabouts two weeks ago."

"Where are you living my son?" enquired the Priest.

"Hell," the lad thought, "this man is no Fr. Ryan."

"I am just down the road, Father," he replied.

"Good," said the Priest, "on with your confession then."

"I have been swearing, Father, but not as much as I used to."

Always a good ploy that, let them know that you are an improved person, that the Church was winning the war against sin, and the sinner. They liked to hear that sort of response, it gave them satisfaction to know that they were being successful and, of course, such an admission could be to the sinner's advantage when the Priest finally got around to giving penance.

"Anything else, my son?" enquired the Priest.

"Here goes," thought the lad and out it came. "I was fornicating, Father."

No immediate response from the Priest, "Good," thought the lad, "he never heard me, that was easy."

Just when he thought that he had cracked it, the Priest spoke. "Was it with Mrs. Murphy at number 24, my son?"

"Oh no, Father, not Mrs. Murphy," said the lad.

"Was it Mrs. Brown then?"

"Ah no, Father," replied the lad.

"Was it Mrs. O'Hara around the corner then?"

"No, Father, and if you don't mind I would rather not tell you the woman's name."

"For your penance, my son, you must do the Stations of the Cross and promise God that you will never fornicate again."

The lad made his responses and left the Confession Box, relieved that he had finally made his peace with God.

As planned the lad went to the side altar where his mate was waiting to hear the news. ''How did it go then?'' his mate asked. ''Not bad at all, that one is no Fr. Ryan and that's for sure. Better get yourself over there quickly. I have some good names and addresses, we will be busy tonight.''

Chapter Six

Nearing the end of my apprenticeship at the Ringsend Dockyard my thoughts were in one direction only, to join the Merchant Service as a junior engineer and to sail the seven seas. I recall my last day there as if it were yesterday.

The boiler tops did not feel as cold that morning, although it was cold. The frozen pools along the cobbled North Wall had reflected my bicycle light at crazy angles as I cycled along. It was most difficult to keep your bike balanced on the North Wall in those days, what with the crane tracks, pot holes and the mounds of horse muck, you needed to be a trick cyclist. The person who got from one end to the other on such a morning without a mishap was a very good cyclist indeed. Many a fall I had, in particular on the wooden cobbles that used to be in the area of Butt Bridge.

I recall negotiating a fast right-hander, pushing hard on the pedals to avoid a horse-drawn cab only to come unstuck in a pile of steaming horse muck. If only polythene bags had been available then, drivers could have cellotaped one under the horse's tail so that when the horse lifted his tail to crap it would have been deposited in the bag and not on the road. Freshly packed horse muck, untouched by human hand, at today's prices I would be a rich man in no time at all.

As I worked that morning I surveyed my surroundings – this by candle light, for that was the method of lighting in those days, either a candle or a duck lamp which used coal oil. Most of my five years at the Dockyard had been spent like this; we were like miners, only above ground. There was a year's deposit of soot and coal dust everywhere. You could go into an engine room that was reasonably clean, but enter the boiler top space and it was another world; it was if that area in some ships did not exist.

Work that morning was a matter of repacking the glands of the valves and grinding the valve seats, not a very interesting job but most important for all that. The usual procedure was to position yourself on one valve, using it as a seat as you worked on another. Each valve had a wheel which was turned clockwise to close the valve and anticlockwise to open it. This detail was denoted by raised lettering, and arrows, on the rim of the valve wheel.

As I sat there that morning, I realised that the nut which bolted the valve wheel to the valve spindle was central to my rectum and that it had some sharp corners which made my position most uncomfortable. I considered this and thought that with the lettering OPEN----SHUT on the wheel, and the mark of the hexagonal nut imprinted on my arse, it was a good job that I was not due for a pile job; otherwise the Doctor would think that I had a detachable ring piece and call for a spanner instead of a scalpel.

This was the day which had been uppermost in my mind for some considerable time, certainly since the Time Snatcher had advised me at the end of the previous month that, as I had lost no time throughout the previous year, there would be no requirement for me to make up for lost time. Yes, strange as it may sound today, all time lost throughout your five-year apprenticeship had to be accounted for annually, and worked out. If, for example, a lad began the first of his five-year stint on September 1st it did not follow that he would commence his second year on the first anniversary of that date. One month prior to the due date, and of course the date when you could, under normal circumstances, look forward to a wage increase, the Time Snatcher would tell you that because you had been absent through the previous eleven months for seven days or whatever you would not commence your second year until you had made good that time.

The reason for your absence was of no consequence to the Dockyard, you had chosen to serve a five-year apprenticeship and so must serve five years and not four and a half or whatever. I broke my ribs at work, this in my third year, and the moment I departed the Dockyard for the hospital my wages stopped. I was absent from work for a full week and returned when still encased in plaster. The time which I lost as a result of that work's accident had to be accounted for at the end of that year.

On an outside wall of the Dockyard some wag had written in large letters ''SLAVE LABOUR'', the epigraph no doubt of some tormented Riveter who had to drift every hole that day and so made but the price of a pint at Tobin's before he took the Corporation Ferry across the Liffy to his home.

Slave labour it was for sure, but what cared I now? Another six hours and I was free. As I ground that valve I thought of another type of grinding, this with a dusky maiden on some sun-kissed beach. Every fibre of my body tingled as I let my thoughts wander, I had never had a sexual relationship, neither had any of my mates. We talked about it for hours and no doubt we would have run a mile had it been offered. Still, we could dream, and dream we did. Now that I was off to sea I would soon experience all these good things, for they say that in the tropics the native girls lie around on the silvery sand waiting for the white man to satisfy their sex-hungry bodies. I was the envy of all my mates as, very soon, I would be part of all that eroticism, whilst they remained at home and just dreamed. How naive we were.

As I worked I reflected on all that had passed, in particular my childhood which had been so wonderful, packed full with all manner of excitement which is sadly missing today. By comparison with modern-day children we had nothing, but of course we were completely unaware of any shortage and therefore never felt deprived. We had the same amount of nothing, the same minus quantity as our playmates, so what was missing? Nothing.

We played endless games each evening after school and when our parents called us for bed we returned home exhausted to climb into bed and sleep the sleep of the just. We had no distractions such as television and video; childhood was for growing up outdoors with your mates, playing the games that our parents, and their parents, had played before us. Indoors was for eating and sleeping and doing school homework.

On summer evenings it was not unusual for parents to join with the children, when dozens would be skipping. A large rope, the full width of the road would appear and fathers would be positioned at either end where they would rotate the rope and all the children would skip. Lines would be formed and it would be "Follow the leader" through the rotating rope. Those who missed their entry would have to drop out of the game, similarly anyone who got caught in the rope.

As the game progressed the rope would turn faster and faster until there was but one person remaining. At this point everyone would scream "Pepper", when fathers would turn the rope as fast as possible. In the end either the "Skipper" jumped "Out" exhausted, or was tripped by the revolving rope.

Another game was "Broken Statues": children would line up in the road and strike a pose, any pose which they felt they could sustain for a period of time, the idea being to mimic a statue. However, some of the comical poses adopted were purely imaginary and the grimaces on faces were indeed a sight.

Now, when everyone had "posed", the "Teacher" would go from "Statue to Statue" and endeavour to get them to smile, laugh, or grin and thereby break their pose, when they would be considered "Out". In attempting to make someone break their adopted pose, the "Teacher" used all manner of tricks, even on occasion going as far as to tickle the "Statue" with a piece of grass under the chin, or pushing the piece of grass up the nostril. All good fun and enjoyed by everyone. On occasion a cry of cheat would be heard, this by someone who felt that they had been treated unfairly. However, such infrequent incidents were played down by the other children who would agree that the "Teacher" had acted properly.

Another game, along similar lines, was "O'Grady Says". Again the "Teacher" would give a command and the participants had to follow the instruction. Typical commands would be "O'Grady Says, Put your hands on your knees", quickly followed by another command to put your hands on your hips, your shoulders, your head, etc. The commands were repeated faster and faster and those who did not follow an instruction were deemed to be "Out".

One game which we played for hours was "I draw a snake behind your back". A semicircle was formed against a hedge or similar and the youngster who was "On" stood against the hedge with his back towards the others, and, his hands joined behind his back with one index finger protruding outwards. His eyes were closed.

One of those in the semicircle would step forward and, speaking the name of the game, "I draw a snake behind your back", would do just that. At this point either that person, or as was more usual, somebody else would touch the outstretched finger and then ask, "Who was that?"

The person who was "On" would turn around and try to guess who it was that had touched his finger. Eyes were the give-away and these were studied to try and establish the culprit. Mates would try and give the nod in every manner of way to assist the searcher and thereby conclude the game, when another would commence.

The favoured way of tipping the nod was by using your feet to point towards the culprit. However, as always some became very sophisticated in this regard and arranged some obscure system of giving the game away. This would require that they pointed to the person second from the left, or the right of the one who was responsible. Of course, for most of the time the plot failed because one or the other forgot the agreed code, when the wrong person would be accused which meant that the game was restarted with the same person being "On".

The era of the one-car family was light years away, the bicycle reigned supreme and the lines of bicycles parked outside Shelbourne Park on race night had to be seen to be believed. They were watched over by men who were self-appointed attendants, wearing official-looking caps with a green band.

As a diversion in later years we would go around to Shelbourne Park with a bicycle spanner and adjust seats, so that those that had been raised to the limit were lowered and those which had been lowered were raised. At times we simply turned the saddle around so that it was pointing backwards, even on occasion just loosened the saddle height nut so that, when the rider placed his bum on the saddle, it immediately dropped to its lowest point.

The fun was when the punters rushed out after the last race, grabbed their bikes and tried to mount. Those of short stature seldom managed to lift their legs high enough to mount their machines, particularly on dark nights when the concern was to beat the rush away from the park. The tall person, having mounted successfully, was equally surprised to sit on the lowered seat with their knees knocking on the bicycle handlebars.

All clean fun; mischievous, yes, but to the best of my knowledge no injury resulted from these pranks. I accept that the cycle owners did not rate our activity as being comical and feel sure that had they caught us then they would have done us a mischief.

Whilst the lads were involved in games such as these, the girls favoured playing with dolls, or hospital and every type of game which was typical of family life. One in particular which I recall the girls playing was "Shop" – simply that, Shop. They would set out a stall with all manner of goods for sale; everything would be arranged in neat rows so that customers could inspect the displayed goods. By way of advertising, and to attract customers, the "Shop" owner would be heard shouting "Buy away, buy away, new shop open, ham, jam, anything you want, M'am."

Looking back, the strangest activity of all was visiting the dead. When a neighbour died at home, our parents would instruct us to go and pay our respects, this by kneeling at their bedside and saying a few prayers. I paid many such visits and marvel at the ease with which we accepted this uniquely Irish custom, this when I was but four years old.

It was not until I was in the Merchant Service that I realised that visiting and praying at the bedside of a dead neighbour was something which was pretty well limited to the Irish. This fact was brought home to me one day when docked at Port of Spain, Trinidad, this perhaps around 1960.

As our ship did not have the luxury of air conditioning and as the weather was extremely hot, we used to go to the Flying Angel Seamans Mission most afternoons to cool off. Approaching one afternoon we noted two hearses complete with coffins outside the building, which sight reminded us that two Radio Officers from a visiting ship had died in a car crash the previous day.

The lady in charge of the Mission, a Londoner, upon seeing us requested our assistance in getting the coffins indoors; speaking up for myself, and as I thought for my companion, our Radio Officer, I replied that we were more than willing to help. We went to the rear of the first hearse as directed and when the coffin was almost out of the hearse, Sparks on one side and myself on the other, we grabbed hold of the handles.

As I was on the righthand side of the coffin and the Mission to my right I paid scant attention to the coffin but concentrated my mind on turning right and heading for the Mission entrance door. Sparks, being on the opposite side of the coffin, as with myself he was concentrating and focusing his attention on turning right. However, in focusing to the right he was in effect looking over the coffin and it was at that point that he collapsed in a faint. Luckily, the man drawing the coffin forward out of the hearse still had hold of it and quickly pushed it back into the hearse.

The reason for Sparks fainting? The coffin was fitted with a glass plate such that the occupant's face was visible and, as he had never seen a dead person before, the shock was too much for him. In fairness I think that the fact that the coffin occupant was a fellow Radio Officer, although unknown, did nothing to help matters.

That last evening, as I came out onto the engine top platform, I heard a commotion below me and looking down I observed one of the ship's engineers directing a couple of greasers in cleaning the engine eccentric strap trough. He was giving them hell because they had thrown the oil-laden water onto the tank tops. "Clean that up before it gets into the bilges," the engineer shouted. The cleaners, typical of this breed of engine-room staff, stared at the engineer with that look which said, "Get stuffed." They turned and got on with the job as directed; in years to come I was to experience that self-same look many times.

The ship was a triple expansion coal-fired steamer built perhaps at the turn of the century. She was a dirty heap and, looking around, I hoped that my first ship would be more presentable. I favoured a steamer, an oil-fired modern triple expansion job with a bright and shiny engine room similar to the Guinness ships, where all the nuts around the cylinder heads shone and the brass edging on the casing gleamed. Yes, such a ship would suit me. However, I wanted deep sea trade, tropic isle sailing, for there were no dusky maidens on the Dublin–Liverpool route.

Packing my tools in a sack (a sack was the forerunner of today's fancy tool box) I made my way back to the Dockyard for the last time, my five-year stint over. I was free.

Mother was not happy that I was leaving the nest, but then mothers are never happy to see their youngsters depart. That is part of their chemistry and the cross that they bear. There were plenty of tears and many requests that I should reconsider and get a job locally, at least for a couple of months when everyone was quite sure that, come that time, I would realise that I had done the right thing. Mother had enlisted the help of her brother Paddy to assist her in pouring cold water on my plans, but the more they tried the more adamant I became: sea it was and nothing would deter me.

I understood my mother's reasons for not wanting me to go; having been widowed but a couple of years, the presence of her children was more essential that ever. However, given that I had assured her of my financial support, I felt it an imposition that she should deny me that which I had set my heart on for so long. Money was tight, my departure, which in turn would mean more free cash within the home, should have been welcomed rather than the reverse. As I saw it, there would be more money each week and, of course, one less mouth to feed.

As always, we make an argument to suit our immediate needs, in the full knowledge that come tomorrow we may sing a different tune. Such is life, always was, and, as night must surely follow day, always will be. So it was that I departed Dublin for Liverpool, where I was engaged as a junior engineer for a ship which was docked in Hamburg.

Chapter Seven

Leaving home and, of course, Dublin was all too easy, for that parting had been the only objective for so many years, the driving force to my existence. As the ferry slipped her mooring ropes and moved to the centre of the Liffy to begin the trip to Liverpool, many passengers lined the rails looking shorewards waving to their loved ones. With few exceptions, all were of heavy heart and one could almost feel the sadness.

I was one of the exceptions, no wet eyes for me. I made my way below deck to secure a comfortable seat as close as possible to the bar. My thoughts were only for that which lay ahead. The sight of Dublin dipping below the horizon was of no interest now, the umbilical cord had been severed, it was off with the old and on with the new.

How our thinking changes. On sailing visits home today I am first on the deck, my eyes scanning the horizon for sight of the Wicklow mountains, my silent voice crooning, "I'm coming home, I've done my time." As the mountains rise out of the sea I know that very soon I will be able to see the twin smoke stacks of the Pigeon House Power Station. The arms of Dublin Bay wait to enfold me, I see the Halfmoon Swimming Club and recall chilly swims of yesteryear. I am once again a young boy baiting my fishing line and hoping for the big one.

Oh, sweet, sweet youth, you have deserted me.

I now depart Dublin heavy of heart, no racing below deck to secure a seat close to the bar. I share the after deck with the flag staff and the seagulls and, as the Dublin Mountains sink below the horizon, I offer a prayer to my Mate above that soon, very soon, my favourite city will rise again, when I will know that I am home.

Leaving Dublin was a dream come true, my years of waiting were over, I was on my way to set the world alight. The fetters were off, and so was I. The oppressiveness of the Church which was so evident at that time, and which virtually controlled our lives, slipped easily off my shoulders and was soon forgotten. I could think all the thoughts which hitherto had been taboo, the Confessional was of another age, no more Saturday fears for I had never seen a tramp ship with a Confession Box – a stuffing box, yes, and this was my aim.

What had I left behind? What was Dublin like in those days and how did the young blades pass their time? Well, unemployment was unheard of, I never knew anyone who did not have a job to go to, although the Dockyards worked on the "hire and fire" principle, that is to say that, when the job was completed, you went up the road; the people concerned usually went from the Ringsend Dockyard to the Liffey Dockyard or even finished one day and were started again two days later on a different ship at the same Dockyard.

As a general rule weekday nights were pretty quiet and, unlike today where everyone meets at the pub every night, such visits with us were limited to the weekend, and even then, by comparison with today's youngsters, visits were of a short duration.

We met at each other's homes or, as was most likely, gathered at the corner of Derrynane Gardens and Bath Avenue, the favourite meeting place where we would sit on the wall of Barr's garden and put the world to rights. Unlike youngsters of today, we were never bored and, although we were no angels, we never vandalised property, snatched handbags or did any of the wicked things which are sadly the norm today.

Our worst behaviour was pinching apples, or as was said in Ireland, "Boxing the fox", but in doing this we were most selective and only took apples when they were ripe and ready to eat. We liked nothing better than a good chase, thinking up all manner of ways to get someone after us, well aware of the fact that, were we caught, we would get a good hiding. Knocking hats off was a favoured way of being chased. We were, however, selective, only picking on the younger males who looked fit enough to run after us. A clear passage was assured for all females, as indeed it was for the older male; respect was something of which we had plenty. One of the gang, Gerry, thought up a sure fire way of getting chased, and also of getting the mother and father of a hiding should you be caught. However, getting caught never entered our heads. We were fleet of foot and, of course, we had the benefit of knowing exactly where we were going and which gardens we could cut across to evade and baffle the chaser.

When the "victim" had been selected, this on the strict understanding that he should be a reasonably fit male, it was simply a question of snatching the man's hat and making a hasty departure. I suppose that in our selection we erred on the side of caution in that we chose a person who was only, or at least appeared to be only, reasonably fit, we wanted the chase to be very much in our favour, it was a question of nearly be caught as opposed to getting a good hiding. Clearly the chaser could not follow everyone and as we sped away in every direction he was left to ponder who it was that actually had the hat.

Now, as a general rule the poor person was so dumbfounded that he seldom if ever reacted immediately and, by the time that the full impact of what had happened to him had sunk in, he just had time to notice us race around the first corner. The next stage of this game would depend on the man and, to some degree on the quality of his hat and the weather conditions. We would observe him from some vantage position and react to the situation as it developed.

Straight away the person would head for the corner of Bath Avenue Gardens, where he had seen the main band of lads disappear. His turn of speed would be assessed on his approach to the corner, and Gerry would act accordingly.

Should the man prove to be athletic and reach the corner in double quick time, we had several options open to make good our escape. Down Mrs. Burke's path and over her back wall into the sportsfield, through Larrigan's, across our garden and out through the front gate to disappear in the direction from which the chaser had come. Finally, run like the wind straight up Bath Avenue Gardens (100 yards) dropping the hat as we went.

Now, as I said earlier, the quality of the hat and the weather conditions came into play at this point. Had it been raining and the road were wet, also were his hat a good one, then what usually happened was that he would pick up his hat, dust it off and decide to call off the hunt. When this happened we would commence to cat-call after him in the hope that we could rekindle his interest. On occasion we did; however, because we had such a good start the interest usually waned after a few minutes.

I recall one particular evening when we were all at the corner eating apples which had been "obtained" from one of our usual sources. Now, one of the gang bit into an apple which was not up to expectations and, seeing a likely "victim" cycling along the other side of the road, decided that what was needed to brighten events was a good chase.

As a general rule, when we wanted some action everyone was alive to the situation, all of one mind as it were, and several pairs of eyes selected and decided on who was to be the "victim". Not so in this instance, one person alone knew that a chase was going to be set up.

The apple was thrown with some considerable force and what happened could well have had serious consequences. The apple hit the poor man on the temple, knocking him off his bike at which moment all hell broke loose. We scarpered every which way and went to ground – and, in my case, that is exactly what I did. Dashing into Bath Avenue Gardens, I literally threw myself under the hedge at old Mrs. Smith's, where I lay for some considerable time listening to the man threatening death on us should he catch us.

Although the man could not see me from the road, old Mrs. Smith would, should she look out of her front window to see what all the commotion was about. I lay there hugging that earth like earth has never been hugged before, praying that Mrs. Smith would not look out, or that if she did, she would conclude that we were simply playing hide and seek or some other childish game.

Eventually the man went away and very gingerly we reassembled. However, we stayed well away from that particular corner for a while, just in case the cyclist decided to follow the same route in the hope that he would recognise and catch one of us.

A winter "occupation" was knocking on the doors of suitable houses which more or less guaranteed to result in a chase. On occasion we even tied a cord to two adjacent knockers, went across the street into the darkness, rattled the knockers and awaited results.

All the houses in the area had iron gates which were hung on two pintles; although these gates were reasonably heavy, two people could lift them off the pintles. Now, one night when it was my turn to rattle the knocker of a known "chaser" in Bath Avenue, the gate was held open for me to do my dirty deed. However, during the time that it took me to get to the door and give the knocker a good rattle, the gate was removed from its pintles and, instead of being kept open to assist my escape, it was closed and I was told to vault the wall.

I did as instructed and, collecting myself on the road side, I noted the owner of the house dashing down his path breathing flames. When he reached the gate he made to throw it open, at which time it fell under his feet and he went bum over bosom to measure his length on the pavement. As we disappeared we could hear him screaming blue murder after us. He was a very athletic young man and I feel sure that, had he caught one of us, he would have killed us. He was badly shaken so he did not immediately follow us; however, it was possible that he might tour the area after he got his wind back, so I had an early night.

We were mischievous and always seeking ways in which we could get some able-bodied person to chase after us. Beyond that, and by comparison with youngsters of today, we were angels. Although we had nothing, we never complained because we were all in the same boat; we made the most of that which we did have and were quite happy that we had the greatest blessing of all, life.

In 1947 there was snow the likes of which had not been seen for years. Everywhere was snowbound for a few days, not, however, the Ringsend Dock-yard and as I lived just along the road I went off as usual. The conditions there were really unbelievable and particularly so for those who were working on a dead ship with no heating. Each morning our tools were frozen solid beside the job on which we had been working the previous day and had to be thawed before we could use them. Did you not follow this procedure for spanners, etc., you ran the risk of having the jaws snap off. In those days you had to supply your own tools so they were treated with respect, and never misused.

As you would expect, we got up to all manner of antics with the snow, rolling large snowballs in front of people's gates so that the residents could not get out – this usually late at night when they were all indoors. Every age group joined forces on one particularly large snowball which, at the appropriate time, was rolled in front of the No.52 bus which ran along Bath Avenue in those days.

The bus stopped at the corner of Derrynane Gardens and Bath Avenue to allow passengers to get off/on. When it was stopped the huge snowball was rolled out of Derrynane Gardens to the front of the bus, where its size came above the driver's line of vision. As usual we all ran off to observe from a safe distance and were not surprised when we noted that the bus could not proceed, and that the combined efforts of the driver and the conductor could not shift the snowball.

Help eventually came and the snowball was broken up with large fire axes and removed from the front of the bus, allowing it to proceed on its journey. All this to loud cheers from the massed gang of lads on the opposite side of the road.

We also went along the railway line from Landsdown Road to gain a position directly above Bath Avenue and from this vantage point we pelted the poor people below with snowballs. During one such outing, when the snow was falling quite heavily and many people were using umbrellas to protect them-selves, one of the gang dropped a snowball, which was perhaps twelve inches in diameter, right onto an umbrella, nigh on flattening the poor person below.

Returning home later, I found my mother's sister in the house and playing merry hell about some uncharitable lout who had dropped a snowball on her from the railway bridge.

At the time that I began my apprenticeship in the Dockyard the practice of apprentice initiation was the only highlight of a very dull day. There were dozens of us and more than anyone the junior apprentice lived in fear of the senior apprentice. He was god. The Foreman held less power, and we walked in fear, dreading the day that we would be set upon and initiated. The senior apprentice would put out the word that you were to be "done" and that was it.

It was not sufficient that you were "done" in one department; you were fair game for each section, each wanted their share of you, each had their own brand of initiation and you had to have them all if you were to be considered a true apprentice.

In the Boilershop, you were sent to the pattern loft on some pretext. This you entered by going up a set of open stairs and, once there, you were immediately surrounded by a gang of apprentices and bundled to the floor. The senior apprentice, who was in charge of operations, stood to one side as you were spreadeagled on the wooden floor and at the appropriate time stepped forward and proceeded to nail you to the floor, this through the shoulders and sleeves of your coat. Your pants and underpants were pulled down around your ankles and nails driven through these to leave you securely fixed to the floor.

By this time the most hardened would be in tears and promising to do anything required if only they would release him. All this fell on deaf ears, as surely as night followed day; so too would your initiation follow. You had to be "done", it was the way of things.

So it was that my manhood was painted with red lead, then covered with putty and finally small pieces of coke were pushed into the putty. Another coat of paint, a loud cheer from the assembled apprentices who immediately departed leaving me transfixed on the floor. I don't recall how long they left me there. However, eventually an apprentice arrived with a claw hammer to remove the nails and release me.

I cleaned myself as best I could. However, my underclothes were ruined and I was concerned with what my mother would say when she saw the mess. I need not have worried because my Uncle Willie, mother's brother, worked at the Dockyard and, knowing what had happened, he was at home when I arrived and he had told her all about my ordeal.

I was also initiated by the Shipwrights. This occurred when I was sent to collect something or other. As soon as I opened the door I realised that I had been set up. I was set upon and thrown into the sawdust pit situated beneath a large saw, the trap door was closed and the saw started when those above began to cut wood. This was a frightening experience because you could see nothing, and the noise and the dust which assailed your nostrils was very scary; you were released after ten minutes.

At Ringsend, at a point where the Corporation ferry landed passengers at the slipway, the confluence of the Dodder and the Liffey, a regatta was held on the first Saturday in August each year. Everyone joined in with local business owners entering teams for the various competitions. There were rowing fours, eights, sculling and all manner of boat races for skiffs and working boats.

As you would expect, the Dockyard featured in most races and competition was strong to be included in a team, practice was essential and, unless you were prepared to attend the training sessions which were every other night in July, you could forget about gaining a place.

Also featured was the greasy pole, perhaps fifteen foot long, at the end of which a large ham was suspended. This was mounted not on dry land but from the deck of a barge moored in the river and, as a result of the activity on the river and the current, the pole mounted horizontally from the deck over the water would seldom be steady but bobbing up and down, making it nigh on impossible for competitors to succeed in getting along the pole to secure the ham.

I think that at the start of the day's activity the charge for attempting the pole was a penny. However, as the day progressed and the ham was still unclaimed, the charge was waived and when this happened there was a constant queue of people anxious to win the prize. Competition was fierce and there was much shoving and pushing, also there were those who would attempt to add to the motion of the barge by rocking it back and forth when they spotted a likely winner on the pole. As a rule the ham was the last thing to be won and this late in the evening when little or no grease remained on the pole.

Other annual events were the Tramps' Ball and the Charladies' Ball which were held in the Mansion House in Kildare Street. These were a must. We all entered into the spirit of things and on occasion, even going to the extent of hiring costumes from Gings in Dame Street. It was not necessary to dress as either a tramp or a char, although many did. My last such ball saw me dressed as a spiv in a gaudy checked suit with wide shoulders and a large cap, a right plonker as they say in modern parlance.

O'Connell Street at that time had several Ice Cream Parlours where you could obtain the most fantastic ice cream creations imaginable. The Palm Grove, Cafollas, The Pillar and others were favourite meeting places when we were flush, usually on a Sunday afternoon. A special of mine was a Knicker-bocker Glory at the Palm Grove; it was about ten inches tall and it took a good half hour to work through, ending with the juices being swigged from the glass. As we used to say, ''Yum Yum, Pigs Bum.''

Our mode of transport was Shanks pony, or, the bicycle. My first and only bike was a twenty-four-inch New Hudson with no gearing, a sturdy little machine which took me all over the city and around most of Wicklow where we went camping. A popular camping spot was along the Avonbeg river at a place called Clara, which featured as the smallest village in Ireland, with half a dozen houses at most, a shop which was also the Post Office, and a Church. Yes, strange as it may be, there was no pub, and in Ireland this in itself must be something of a record.

I retraced my steps to Clara in September a few years ago and was most surprised, but extremely pleased, to see that the place was as I had left it after my last camp there in July 1949. The shop was gone; however, in all other respects, the place was the same, a colour change to the paintwork of the house by the bridge perhaps, but the peace and quiet were just the same. No concrete monstrosity to assault the eye here, the planner is banned from this secluded haven and a good job too.

The distance, Derrynane Gardens to Clara, is perhaps forty miles and when you consider that we carried all our camping equipment and that the bicycles had no gearing, the journey was quite an arduous one. However, by comparison with a similar journey today with all the traffic congestion, our parents did not have to worry that we might be knocked down by a car. Once we had passed along the river Dargle by Bray, a car was indeed a rare sight.

Chapter Eight

In the late forties elections were a regular feature in Dublin and each political party held open air meetings at which, as ever, each promised the world if you would put an X by their candidate's name on your voting paper. Large stages were erected in the road and from these platforms many lies were spoken; nothing changes.

These meetings were always well attended and there was much heckling of the speakers, such as "You're so crooked you can't lie straight in bed", "Who stole the harness off the nightmare?" and many other less polite remarks. We joined in this barracking, indeed in many instances we started it and kept it up until we were chased away. We would dash off, giving the impression that we were away for good, but not at all: we would regroup and return to another side of the platform where we would start all over again.

After father's death, finances were such that in an effort to make ends meet mother took in lodgers. One of these, a Carlon man, stayed with us for perhaps three years, during which time he and I became close friends. He was an organiser for one of the political parties with a responsibility to prepare for, and arrange, Party meetings throughout Counties Meath and Kildare. As he was not keen on travelling alone to the various places that his work required him to attend, he usually invited myself and my close friend George McLoughlin to join him.

He was very much a man of the world; a union activist when working as a fitter at some country factory his potential as a capable organiser for the Party was quickly recognised. Like so many before him, indeed as ever was and ever will be, he soon adapted to his new-found life style and the factory floor problems which had aided his climb aboard the gravy train were soon forgotten. "Yes, brother, I hear you, have faith in me, I am working very hard to ease your lot, be patient."

Having had the opportunity to examine the other side of the fence and having enjoyed the cream, he was now more than ever fully aware that there was not sufficient cream for everybody; he was, however, satisfied that he was aboard and was quite prepared to pull the ladder in. He was a likable rogue who was soon ahead of the game in terms of self help, if it could be fiddled he knew how, and to what degree.

On occasion a colleague of his would join us and to hear that pair plotting and scheming was an education. George and myself would sit quietly on the back seat, avid listeners hanging on to their every word, marvelling that, by comparison with those two, we were dumb in the extreme. When either of the duo mentioned something which should not have been uttered in our presence, we would be instructed to forget anything we might have heard; on such occasions we would enquire, "Hear what?"

His colleague was a rather large man with a swarthy complexion and a hooked nose who was, we had been informed, the product of a union between an Irishman who had been part of the Klondyke gold rush and a squaw of unknown tribe. Whilst I cannot vouch for the truth of the foregoing I can say that I would not doubt that which was given to me as being fact; the man's features did resemble those of a Red Indian, he was of an age where his father could well have been at the Klondyke.

Upon arrival at wherever the Carlow man was required to organise something, my friend and I would walk around the town, weigh up the local talent and perhaps call into a cafe for a cup of tea. At a previously arranged time we would meet up with our friend when we would retire to some drinking house for a couple of jars. Occasionally it was obvious that, whereas this was most definitely our first and only drink, the same could not be said of our driver and one night, when at a place in Co. Meath, this fact was more than clear.

It was an extremely cold and frosty night; it was foggy and the road was like a skating rink. In spite of his condition our friend insisted that he would drive, nothing we said would make him alter his thinking; the conditions, he said, were far too dangerous for amateurs, "get in the back of the car and shut up" was his final word on the matter, so off we set from Edenderry with a slightly inebriated driver.

Nearing Chapelizod on the outskirts of Dublin and upon rounding a slight bend three cyclists appeared in the road ahead of us; one cyclist was central in the road whilst the other two wobbled along on either side. The speed with which our driver reacted to the situation left us in no doubt that, whereas he had certainly had more than a few jars, his reflexes were quite good. However, road conditions being as they were, also the positions of the cyclists were such that we stood no chance, with the result that we collided with the cyclist who had chosen the central road position. The driver wrestled with the wheel to prevent the car from ending up in the ditch and eventually we came to a halt.

We quickly scrambled out of the car when we realised just how bad conditions were; the road was so slippery that we had great difficulty in walking, it was a coal black night and this, coupled with the fog, did not help as we made our way back along the road. The scene which we came upon was frightening, one man was lying in the road crying, ''Jasus, I'm dying'', the other pair were trying, with little success, to console him.

It would be fair to say that George and myself were very much out of our depth, we were very frightened and, for my part, I had no doubts whatsoever, I would be in the Dock as an accomplice to murder; as I viewed our situation, the injured man was at death's door, why else would he be making peace with his maker? Although our speed had not been great we had hit him with some force so it was possible that he was Heaven bound, or wherever.

The three cyclists were uniformed soldiers who had been out on the town and were pretty drunk; they had, I suppose, travelled that road in a similar condition many times without incident, certainly they had no lights but then did any cyclists outside the City have lights at that time?

Our driver, in weighing up the situation, was quick to point out to the trio that their reckless cycling, with no regard for other road users, had endangered our lives; they had, he said, been very irresponsible and he would see that the incident was brought to the attention of the proper authority.

The most urgent requirement was to get the injured soldier off the road and into hospital; the first question, however, was which hospital, and where was it in relation to our current location? Unlike a similar occurrence today, where by that time dozens of vehicles would have arrived at the scene, also the ubiquitous cellphone, not one car, bike or otherwise was to be seen, we were very much alone and miles away from any communication facility; the onus was ours to get the injured man to hospital. One of the soldiers said that there was a hospital in Phoenix Park and more important, he knew the way there.

George and myself got onto the rear seat and the injured man, still screaming that death was upon him, was positioned across our knees; the soldier who supposedly knew the route to the hospital got into the front along with the driver and so we set off from the scene of the accident.

It soon transpired that the navigator had no idea of where the hospital was. I think that his only concern had been to get into the car and get warm. The injured soldier took to crying that he did not want to go to hospital, whereupon I piped up saying that it was I and not him who was going to hospital. Finally, at about 2.00 a.m. we did manage to get to a hospital and, depositing the two soldiers, we made our way home, or so myself and George thought.

Not so. Our driver stated that we must go back to Chapelizod and report the accident to the Police there, as failure to do so could have serious consequences. We were not very pleased with this arrangement as by that time it had turned 3.00 a.m. and, unlike our driver who was pretty much a free agent, we would have to attend work at 8.00 a.m., in five hours' time to be precise.

However, we had no choice in the matter, so off we set for Chapelizod in weather conditions that surely resembled the Arctic. We were tired, cold and hungry, but above all we were apprehensive as to the outcome and, in particular, we were concerned that we would be required as witnesses. Although we were satisfied that our driver was blameless in that he had been driving correctly, we knew that he had taken a number of drinks.

The "Blow in the Bag" days were light years away, drink and drive was a way of life. How was the car owner to get home if he was banned from driving simply because he had taken a few drinks? "I can drive better when drunk" was very much an acceptable statement, this because having had a few drinks, and being aware of this, the driver addressed the road and other road users in a more cautious manner. The risk of accident was therefore greatly reduced: at least, that was the drinkers' reasoning, the truth would come in thirty years.

The first task when we reached Chapelizod was to locate the Police Station. This was to prove more difficult than we would have imagined in that it was 4.00 a.m., icy cold, foggy and there was nobody about to answer our enquiries.

Eventually we did find the Police. However, it was a house rather than a station and, knock as we did, we could get no answer. There were lights within so we persisted until finally the door was opened by a bleary-eyed Police Sergeant. There was no immediate invitation to enter the building, we were kept on the doorstep until the driver had explained the reason for such a late visit; finally we were allowed into the office/room when we made our way to the blazing fire which we had observed from the door.

Clearly, the Sergeant was on duty, or should have been on duty. The fact that he had inbibed was also very evident. The driver gave a full account of what had happened, emphasising that the three soldiers had been riding bicycles without lighting, riding in a manner which virtually blocked the thoroughfare to other users, and also that the three were the worst for drink. When asked, both George and myself gave statements which supported what the driver had said.

Paper work completed, the Sergeant surprised us by stating that he would have to request that the driver take him out in the car to check the car's braking capability. To say that we were dumbfounded would be an understatement. The roads were treacherous, a skating rink and this fool wanted to test the brakes.

George and I again took the back seat whilst the driver and the Sergeant got in the front. The Sergeant had another surprise for us; turning to the driver he stated, ''Sure I'm glad to note, sir, that you have not been drinking.'' This, we later agreed, to cover his own transgressions and supporting our belief that the Police Station-cum-House should have been open when we arrived.

Some months later we each received a summons to appear at Kilmanaham Court as prosecution witnesses. Again Paddy's worldly wise ways came to our rescue as neither George nor I had any knowledge of such matters. ''Don't worry'' was his constant reminder to us; if asked to detail what had happened on the night in question, simply repeat what we had said to the Police Sergeant at Chapelizod.

Very easy, Paddy; but what did we say? So we then set about trying to remember the exact detail of the incident and, if possible, to recall exactly what words we had used to relate this to the Sergeant. Whereas Paddy then set about forgetting the entire business, on the back-burner as it were until required, the two of us spent hours testing each other to ensure that we were well versed in the detail of that evening.

When we pointed out to Paddy that we would be losing a day's pay at least in attending Court his response was the usual, ''Don't you worry'; again he demonstrated that he was alive to all situations. Thereupon he explained that, as prosecution witnesses, we would be paid for our time and for all travel expenses, perhaps even a meal. The picture began to take on a more acceptable colour and, come the dreaded day, we went to Court with a detailed but inflated account of our expenses.

The soldiers were charged on three counts, driving without lights, driving without consideration and finally driving whilst drunk. We were never called to give a statement as they had admitted all charges, for which they were fined one shilling (five pence) on each charge.

After the hearing we went to the Clerk of the Court, who questioned us on our expenses, suggesting that perhaps we could get into work for half a day; it was only noon, he pointed out. Paddy again came to our rescue, stating that although it was only noon we would have to return home first and change into our working clothes, then have our dinner and, as it would take us at least an hour just to get home, we most certainly could not attend work. We were paid the full amount claimed and left the Court well pleased with our day's work.

Whilst there was no I.R.A. activity that would equate with, nor resemble, anything that is today's norm, there were nonetheless activists who were very much underground. I don't know what they did or whether or not they did anything; certainly they were about and to the best of my knowledge they were hounded out at every opportunity. At about 8.00 a.m. one morning all hell broke out in Derrynane Gardens when the Police raided the home of a very well-respected family, one of whom was a Nun who was at that time in the house. Knowing exactly what they were after, the Police went quickly about their business and shortly after entering the house they were dragging the handcuffed son of the house towards the Police car.

The onlookers, and there were many, were very surprised because this particular family were a well-respected part of what was a close-knit community. They were, it was thought, the least likely to have had any connection with anything unsavoury; the daughter had taken Holy Orders, therefore it was felt they were above any involvement with the I.R.A. or suchlike.

Shocked as we were, nobody would have credited what followed had they not witnessed it with their own eyes. The son was bundled into the Police car, which immediately sped off with the Nun hard after it screaming, ''Heil, Hitler!'' In today's parlance, we were ''gob smacked''. The incident was the talk of the neighbourhood for weeks, the eighth wonder of the world as it were.

The City Morgue was at that time sited on the River Dodder adjacent to No. 77 Derrynane Gardens, and this offered a very morbid pastime for those with a stomach for looking at dead bodies which had been fished from the river and other such places. Whilst it was not a must as far as I was concerned, I did visit there on several occasions and witnessed the caretaker swill the bodies down with a hose pipe.

The caretaker appeared to delight in watching us peer through the open door and, as a rule, he would invite us to enter and take a closer look at the body on the slab.

I recall seeing the body of a local woman there. She had been fished from the Liffey and her husband was thought to have thrown her off the Halfpenny

Bridge. He was a local from the Irishtown area and it was well known that there were marriage difficulties which had resulted in separation; divorce was unheard of in Ireland in those days.

The separation procedure as I understand it, that is in terms of finances, was that the husband would attend some office or other and hand in his weekly maintenance money. The wife also attended the same office to collect the said money and it was likely therefore that an estranged couple did, on occasion, pass each other during the process.

The last sighting of the woman in question was after she had collected her money, this very shortly after the husband had deposited same with whatever authority. The account was that she left the office and was seen to walk onto the Halfpenny Bridge to cross the Liffey. It was a foggy evening with limited visibility; the next sighting was the following morning when her body was found in the river.

She had been a respected lady who had suffered considerably throughout her marriage. She had, it was said, put up with all manner of hardship since marrying that rotter of a husband. The truth is unknown to me. However, as far as the local women were concerned, he was as guilty as hell.

The story as told was that, having paid in the maintenance money and, knowing the route which his wife took required that she crossed the river, he positioned himself in the centre of the bridge in the hope that, at the appropriate time, she would be the only person on it. It had been a foggy evening so everything was in his favour, certainly nobody else had been around other than the witness who had seen her step onto the bridge. Yes, the local women felt, he had thrown her into the river, and now the rotten bastard must hang.

He was arrested on suspicion of murder and brought to the morgue under Police escort to identify the body. The roadway outside was lined with screaming women who, given the slightest opportunity, would have strung him up there and then. I don't recall the outcome of this incident, so can't confirm the truth or otherwise of the man's guilt; sufficient to say that the affair brightened up a dull day.

Another bright feature was the arrival once a year or thereabouts of the tinker family who mended umbrellas, pots and pans, etc. They would set up stall in Derrynane Gardens and it was fascinating to watch them at work, particularly when they would make and fit a complete new bottom to a pot, all this without solder or rivets.

The procedure was that the bottom was cut away from the defective pot, the edge of the wall of the pot was then flanged. The prepared pot was then placed on a sheet of tin and a metal scribe used to mark the exact shape of the flanged pot bottom onto the tin plate. Using a tin shears, the worker proceeded to cut the tin plate so that the eventual diameter of the required piece of tin was six mm greater than the flange mark.

Now the skill of these people came to the fore. With the help of a small hammer, and an anvil, the new bottom was folded over so that the six mm outer area was perhaps 100 degrees from the flat, this for almost half of the total circumference. The previously flanged pot was then placed on the new bottom, the flange being inserted into the folded edge, which was then closed completely over it.

Using a small hand anvil and a hammer the joint was hammered flat. When this situation was achieved, the newly formed joint was folded through ninety degrees to lie flat against the side of the pot. The craftsman then worked deftly around the circumference with the anvil and his small hammer to ensure that a secure seal was created between the pot and the newly formed bottom.

The only problem with this method of repair was that the pot was now six mm less in depth than when the job was commenced. A further minus factor was that the tin used was inferior and as a consequence the life expectancy of the repaired article was considerably reduced.

Chapter Nine

Like all major cities, Dublin, although the capital of a Catholic country, had its fair share of prostitution and the "ladies of the night" plied their trade quite openly. At least, it appeared to be quite open in that we knew exactly where to go and observe the comings and goings of those who sought their pleasures outside the marital bed.

A favourite spot for the "knee trembler brigade" was an unlit lane off Bachelor's Walk in the city centre. We used to frequent a dance hall in that area every Saturday night and, although passing along this lane was a little off our direct and better illuminated route, we took a delight in cycling along without lights, but with the cycle lamp ready in our hand.

The plan was to cycle along the lane and, when your eyes had adjusted to the darkness, you could see the location of a "lady" and her customer in a doorway along the wall. Once located they were fair game and pressing hard on the pedals we would flash our lights on the couple. As a rule there was little or no response from the pair in action. However, most nights there would be an orderly queue of customers on the opposite wall awaiting their turn. Perhaps some were not waiting their turn at all but got their kicks from watching the action. Whichever, it was always this group of men who shouted at us to "Turn that light out and clear off"; this we did whilst cat-calling, "You dirty old bastard."

There were several women who worked the ships and these we saw regularly when working out along the quays. We got to know them and there was friendly banter whenever we met up, this either aboard some ship, along the quays or perhaps on the Corporation ferries which plied the river from north to southside.

Most of those I recall were truly whores in every sense of the word. They were slovenly, unkempt women who were past their best and one would have to be quite desperate even to contemplate approaching them. I particularly recall a small dumpy "lady" who wobbled along the cobble-stoned quay, a pair of broken-down shoes on her feet, and a tatty coat draped across her shoulders.

A group of us were returning to the Dockyard one afternoon when some way ahead of us, walking in the general direction of a ferry point, were two "ladies", one of whom was the dumpy one. As always on such occasions, we increased our pace to catch up with the pair and enter into dialogue with them. One of our party, more anxious than the rest of us to get into conversation, started to heckle the pair. It was obvious that they were not in their usual jovial mood because, looking behind and seeing us, they glowered, making it pretty obvious that they were not of a mind for friendly banter. The signs were clear, business was bad, or there was no business at all.

Undeterred, our hero persisted with his comments. The rest of us, fearing that matters could get out of hand, slowed our pace until we had virtually stopped, by which time our hero was ahead of us. Engaged as he was in taunting the pair, he was totally unaware that we had separated from him and that he was now alone, and by that time, pretty close to the "ladies". The pair stopped walking, turned around and the dumpy one lifted her skirts, saying as she did so, "Come on, son, do you want a bit?" Our hero, realising that he was now alone, was rooted to the spot; ashen-faced, he did not know which way to turn. He got no support from us because we were urging him to take up the offer, adding that, were he short of funds, we would copper up to help him out.

The pair entered into the fun of the occasion; the boot was certainly on the other foot. They had the advantage and really gave our hero a rough time of it. The incident eventually ended when we all made our way to the ferry, mates again, each making a living out of shipping.

Working very late one night on a ship on the North Wall, myself and my mate went into the galley to have a hot drink. It was perhaps midnight. We were alone for ten minutes or so when the Donkeyman came in one door, crossed the length of the galley, and went out the other door. In passing he nodded to us and that was it, at least that was what we thought.

The Donkeyman had no sooner gone out one door than "Dumpy" came in the other and enquired from us if we had seen the Donkeyman. "Yes," we replied, "he has just gone out that door over there." "Thanks," she said, and clip-clopped across the galley, out the door and away after the Donkeyman. We looked at each other wondering what the hell was afoot; clearly something was afoot and we were keen to know what it was all about.

During our speculations we again heard "Dumpy's" by now familiar clip-clop along the steel decking. The clip-clop was getting louder, suggesting that she was returning to the galley. Sure enough, seconds later she entered panting and gasping for breath and, seeing that she was all in, we invited her to sit awhile and take a drink of tea.

Sitting down, she unfolded a story that was at once sad and comical and left us not knowing which way to turn. Certainly neither of us could offer any words of comfort; it was doubtful if we could speak at all.

Her reason for chasing the Donkeyman? Well, it transpired that she had serviced most of the Firemen and Greasers, each had paid for her charms and she had placed the earned money in her tatty purse. Whilst she was engaged at her trade on a bunk with one or another of the crew, the Donkeyman had stolen her purse.

Dumpy, as we had named her, was indeed a pathetic, beaten little person who gained little pleasure from her passage through life. Did she not follow the world's oldest trade, where, and how, would she make ends meet? Free state handouts as we know them today were unheard of, the "Freebie" era had yet to arrive.

As I have said, her story was both sad and comical. As the Yanks would say, "She worked her butt off for nothing." Little wonder that she was annoyed with the Donkeyman for stealing her purse. How many times had this happened before? Certainly I doubt that this was the first occasion that she had been robbed, for the conditions where she worked were quite open to such "bottom of the barrel tricks".

In the main, the ships that they worked were the open forecastle type, port side for the deck ratings and starboard for the engine room gang. There was no privacy other than perhaps a curtain across your bunk; the single cabin status was eons away. The woman would simply go from bunk to bunk, or if there was a spare bunk then she would commandeer that, using it as her "work place". Whichever way she worked, she was vulnerable, and the unscrupulous had the advantage to short change, or rob her.

The going rate at that time was two shillings (tenpence) in the lanes and two shillings and sixpence (twelve and a half pence) in a bunk aboard ship. Those rates were constant for a number of years because in 1953, when docked at Custom House Quay, Cork, in Southern Ireland, I was to experience their method of work at first hand as it were. I hasten to add that I never sampled their charms. I did, however, have a knock on my cabin door and the price asked was two shillings and sixpence.

On a subsequent evening in Cork, when strolling up and down the deck with the Chief Officer, we noted a "working lady" coming up the gangway. It was a spring evening, approaching 9.00 p.m., and as the "lady" stepped aboard my colleague thought that it was time to put a bit of action into the evening.

The Chief Engineer was an elderly, scholarly and deeply religious man who had several relations in the Church. He seldom if ever went ashore, was teetotal and, as you can imagine, most certainly would have nothing to do with prostitution.

Rather than tell the prostitute to get off the ship, which was the usual practice, the Chief Officer approached her and told her that the Chief Engineer would be a very keen and willing customer. He then instructed the "lady" on the location of the Chief's cabin and, being satisfied that she was on the right course, he indicated that we should depart to a position where we could hear, if not observe, the fun without leaving ourselves open for the criticism which would most certainly ensue.

We heard the row which erupted and heard the "lady" scurry along the deck in the direction of the gangway. We also heard the Chief moving around and under the circumstances thought it prudent to remain where we were, lest he put two and two together and came up with the right answer.

In the saloon the following morning, the Chief Engineer was complaining to the Captain about the laxity of the watchman, pointing out that it had quite upset him that a prostitute should be allowed the opportunity to ply her trade in the Officers' quarters. Everyone in the saloon was listening intently to what was being said and, as to my knowledge there were but two people aboard who knew the truth of the situation, there was much tut-tutting.

At this point the Chief Officer entered the saloon and took his seat at the dining table to the right of the Captain, a position which placed him directly opposite the Chief Engineer. All was quiet as the gathered company reflected on the Chief Engineer's experience of the previous evening when, to my utter shock and amazement, the Chief Officer, addressed the Chief Engineer: "Chief, I believe that you had a woman in your cabin last night."

With the exception of the Chief Engineer, those present were stunned to silence. The Chief Engineer changed colour several times, his mouth opening and shutting as he attempted to utter something. When at last he spoke, his words were calm and considered. "Number One," he said, "I'll have you know that none of my sperm entered that woman's body.'' The saloon was hushed.

Although contraception was available it was most definitely not available in Catholic Ireland and pity the person who contemplated such and repented to the Priest. Marriage was for begetting children, Catholic children. ''Dipping the wick'' for pleasure was unthinkable, and a sin in the eyes of the Church. By all means do it, but pray that God will bless the union with another little Catholic baby.

It was said in Ireland at that time that the first thing a newborn baby did was to vacate the womb and make way for another one. The Priest liked to see a healthy young couple produce a baby every year and, did this not happen, questions would be asked in the Confessional. ''Are you sure there is nothing else to confess?'' would be a typical question to either party when they were on their knees in the dark confines of the Confession Box. ''I pray that God will help you in your endeavours and bless your marriage with a child.'' It was a brave person, or a sinner, who ignored the warning. Better to stop the withdrawal method and get him off your back, thinking as he does that you are committing sin every night and flying in the face of God.

The rhythm system was widely used. This required the couple to carefully watch the calendar, the woman's menstruation cycle and several other factors, not least of which was whether or not either party felt inclined. The wags of the day, always alive to make fun of this important topic, quoted the couple who, having carefully noted all the factors, which coincided at 2.00 a.m., were unable to locate a dance band to give them the required rhythm.

As the man said of his member, ''it has to be fed and it's too far from the ground to nibble the grass.'' So it was a baby a year, no sex, Mrs. Hand or the back lane; whichever, it was a sin and should be confessed.

My own grandmother had seven children in as many years, burying the last two before they finally buried her – this and she less than fifty years of age. She was by no means unique; the graveyards of Dublin of the day were full of such women.

My grandfather married again and started fathering once more, three with this wife before she too went to an early grave, a broken woman. He then waited a few years before he went to the altar for the third time, no filly this time, however, but a woman past her child-bearing years who outlived him.

When I started at the Dockyard I got a terrible shock one day when an elderly painter enquired if I was ''Poison Prick's grandson''. Needless to say, I was quite unaware of what was meant by the remark. The man, noting my ignorance, explained in detail what he meant.

Yes, I was indeed a grandson, most unhappy, however, to learn that the local women had branded him a "killer" because two of his wives had died early. Was he not doing what the good Lord required of married men? Or, if not the Lord, then the Priest expected him to father Catholic children as often as possible, so was he to blame that his wife could not stay the course?

Against this background it will be appreciated that there was none of the single parenthood that abounds today, unmarried mothers were almost unheard of. Certainly there were none in the area of Derrynane Gardens and there were several hundred houses in that area. Of all the girls in that locality there was a suspicion that one of them had gotten herself with child, nothing certain, just a suspicion. However, she did go missing for several months. "She has gone to live with her Aunt who is sick and needs some assistance': this was the stock answer which was given when the question was asked as to where she was.

In addition to repairing ships, the Dockyard also contracted for work at any establishment which operated steam raising plant and machinery. We worked in all manner of places, from which I gained invaluable experience.

One particular establishment, where we overhauled the steam generating plant, was run by the Nuns. It was in the area of Clondalkin or Ashtown; the exact location, however, is of little consequence. This convent, Hospice or whatever operated to serve the community by way of providing a place where unmarried mothers could have their babies and depart home, leaving the baby for adoption or similar.

On one occasion there, I was working as apprentice with a chap named Hannigan, a single man of perhaps twenty-six and rather presentable. There was no Boilerman or similar, such work being undertaken by the Nuns; in fact, I rather doubt that there was any work in that establishment which was not carried out by the Nuns.

Having been fully briefed on the exact nature of the work to be undertaken, we set about this upon arrival without ever seeing anyone in authority. We had worked perhaps for a couple of hours when a young Nun appeared in the boiler room, laden down with a pot of tea, milk, sugar and some sandwiches.

To say that Hannigan and myself were struck dumb would best describe our reaction. This Nun was strikingly beautiful; she wore the then newly fashionable rimless glasses, was perhaps in her mid-twenties, and oozed personality and charm. "I thought that you could manage a drink of tea," she said to us, "it's hot work in here." The words were lilted and were music to our ears.

Were she dumb, which she certainly was not, she would still have realised that she had captivated the pair of us. We drooled something about thanks, adding that she was too kind. Under the breath it was "Darling, whatever is a beauty like you doing hiding in a place like this? Will you accompany me to the dance tonight?"

When we had composed ourselves, we got talking with the Nun to learn that she was the boiler attendant, and no boiler has ever been attended by such a lovely creature. When she was away from the boilers Hannigan and I agreed that, if ever a woman was wasted, she was the one; to know that she toiled with a shovel feeding coal into this hungry boiler was too much for us to comprehend – she should be outside bearing children, *my* children.

During our time there we became quite friendly with this Nun and I feel sure that she was aware of our feelings and, indeed, even played us along. At lunchtime we would sit out on the grass and eat our sandwiches; it was summertime and lazing out there for the allowed half hour recharged us to face the afternoon toil.

As I have said, this establishment was run by the Nuns to provide a haven for unmarried mothers. The women went there when they knew they were pregnant and remained there until the child was born, when they would return to their families. Those children who were old enough were taken out daily for a walk around the estate. They were in similar-aged groups, walked in straight lines, and were always in the company of a Nun.

Whilst lying in the grass one day, we noticed a group of four-to-five year-olds coming along towards us with our lovely in charge. We sat up so that we could note her every move and, black habit or not, we just knew that she was a mover; that her body was voluptuous was a certainty – had we not stripped her with our eyes each day since our arrival?

The children changed direction and headed straight towards us, with our darling right behind them. We were going to get a right eyeful of her loveliness.

The first child was level with Hannigan. Ten, a dozen children to pass and it would be her right beside him. He was weak-kneed, it was a good job that he was not required to stand up. The first little voice piped up to Hannigan, "Hello Daddy"; this was the cue, they all spoke to Hannigan as they filed past: "Hello Daddy."

Poor Hannigan was speechless, I was watching the young Nun's face and it was a picture, she was enjoying every minute of this play which she had set up. She stopped by Hannigan and spoke to him, commenting on the weather, her eyes dancing with joy. She had turned the tables and knew that Hannigan did not know how to cope. She turned on her heels, swishing her hips so that the habit lifted above her shoes to reveal a beautifully turned ankle. She was indeed a beauty; God was the lucky one that she had married him and not either of us.

During my time at the Dockyard I worked at many similar establishments and in the process had several experiences which opened my eyes to the Clergy in Ireland at that time.

One place where I worked on several occasions was an establishment where Priests were sent to dry out and be cured of their liking for drink. This experience was to show me that Priests, like the rest of us, were but human and as such subject to the self-same temptations; and that in spite of all their training they could, and indeed did, fall.

I don't say that I gloated at this new-found knowledge. However, my informed position made it more difficult for me to accept that the Priest had the right to stand up in the pulpit in Church and berate us lesser mortals for our weakness. I reasoned that, if they could fall, surely then we also could stray, and perhaps we should not be made to feel too bad about our waywardness. We were all but human and ever likely to sin given a certain set of circumstances; this thinking presupposes that the Priest was not hounded by his superiors for his sins.

Another experience was when I worked at a Blind Asylum which was run by Nuns. Looking back it would appear that all such places were run by the Nuns, telling us, should it require telling, that these are indeed very special people who give their lives unselfishly to God. Bless them all, and I forgive them for taking my dream away and using *her* as a boiler stoker.

The first time that I attended the Blind Asylum was by way of taking a message to a Dockyard colleague. Not knowing the layout I called at the main entrance to enquire the location of the boiler house. Inside the main door was sited a type of kiosk within which sat a little Nun at a desk. Before I reached the service hatch to the front of the kiosk, the Nun enquired if she could help me.

I told her that I was from the Dockyard and that I wished to get to our workers in the boiler house. "I'll take you there," said the Nun as she arose from the desk and came out of the kiosk. She set off at a brisk pace down a corridor and within twenty feet she turned left, then immediately right and straight on once more, around two further corners, then finally she stopped and said that I should proceed through the door opposite and cross the yard. There I would see the Boiler House directly in front of me.

Our passage through the main building was brisk, there was no faltering; when the required corner was arrived at we turned, this at least on four occasions. Initially I wondered why the Nun was clicking her fingers as we passed along the corridors. Finally the penny dropped: the Nun was herself blind and clicking her fingers was the echo-sounding equipment that enabled her to navigate so precisely through those lengthy corridors.

As Nature deprives us of one faculty God, it would appear, strengthens another to compensate for our loss. A very humbling experience, a lesson learnt; be thankful for what you have, there are many less fortunate.

We also worked quite frequently at a biscuit factory. This was a choice job in that there were plenty of girls about. More important, however, you could get your hands on plenty of biscuits if you knew the ropes, and I knew them.

Security at factory gates as evident today was mostly unheard of; certainly the Gateman never bothered us and never searched our equipment. We went in and out untroubled that a Gateman would ask what was in our bags, which was usually nothing anyway.

I had become friendly with a lad who worked there, having met him at dances, and whereas we could not get into the main part of the factory where the finished product was, he could.

A bargain was struck whereby he would supply one tin of best biscuits for each of us in the boiler house – this on the strict understanding that, when getting our boxes off site, we also took one for him and delivered same to his home. This worked like a charm to the benefit of all concerned; however, I had a very narrow escape on one occasion and wondered if it were really worth the trouble and heartache.

One morning the mobile welding set wherein we stashed the loot was required elsewhere, this before we had managed to get the loot away. As the three tins were already in our possession in the boiler house, we had to move quickly. There were no means of getting them back into the factory nor of disposal. There was only one way and that was out the gate on the lorry upon which the welding machine was mounted.

It fell to me to get the stuff away, so it was loaded and off I set to deliver all three boxes to their new homes. Everything went well and I was in the area of Butt Bridge, heading towards Ringsend, when I skidded the lorry into the back of another lorry; nothing serious, mind you, but the other driver was quite unhappy and wanted to involve the Police, the Priest, the Pope, the whole bloody world, whereas my one and only concern was to get away as soon as possible. I should not have been there in the first place, and secondly I still had the loot aboard. He wanted to fully examine his lorry for damage. There was none, and this I think upset him – I had run into him, so there should be damage, OK, so we could see nothing, but perhaps it was where we could not see it, and what then would his boss say? Better that we exchanged business addresses and played safe. He was in the clear then and, should his boss want, he could contact the Dockyard.

By this time a few had gathered around us, each expressing opinions as to what should be done. Both vehicles were examined. When it was finally concluded that there was no damage to his lorry, he was advised to clear off and let the traffic continue. I encouraged this thinking until, at long last, the other chap got into his lorry and drove away. I followed suit a little shaken that the consequences could have been quite serious.

When I finally returned and related the event to my colleagues, they were relieved to learn that all had turned out as it had. We pondered the consequences had the Police become involved, particularly had they found the biscuits, in contemplating such an eventuality the pair enquired, "What biscuits, Donal? We hope that you have not been stealing."

As ever, if there was a can to be carried the burden would rest with the youngest member of the party, the fall guy. In no way were they, tried and trusted tradesmen as they were, involved; the incident was down in total to Donal.

Chapter Ten

Working conditions, indeed every condition, in the Ringsend Dockyard when I started there in 1945 were archaic. I rather doubt that any words of mine could accurately describe them. Were I so lucky that I did manage to capture them in words I suspect that the reader would accuse me of exaggeration or distorting the truth.

The Dockyard had been opened in 1912 by a Scot, one Mr. McMillan, who had resided in Sandymount with his wife and son James who was, as the saying goes, "One sandwich short of a picnic". By the time that I arrived at the Dockyard Mr. McMillan had departed this life and the only family involvement was through the son who, because of the family connection, and his limitations, had been guaranteed a job for life. James was in charge of the Rivet Stores where he reigned supreme, lord and master of all he surveyed; he was alone in a room which was perhaps twenty foot square and kept the door locked at all times.

James was perhaps fifty and, like many of his type, a big man, as strong as a horse, slow of movement and, under normal circumstance, docile. Treated gently and correctly, that is to say, going along with his funny ways (and, my, they were funny) you could get anything out of him; he was like putty and could be moulded to suit the occasion.

As ever, and always, he was not left to get along with his chores but was aggravated at every opportunity to a degree that it was a miracle that he never killed somebody. Unquestionably, had he caught the perpetrator of any of the many pranks that were played on him, he most certainly would have killed him.

His day consisted of sorting rivets, service bolts and plate washers as returned to the Stores upon completion of a repair when a ship had departed one of the dry docks. Each item was carefully sorted and cleaned, bolts and nuts were oiled and, if necessary, a die was run down the bolt to ensure that the threads were not damaged.

All this work was carried out at a work bench and the restored item was carefully placed into an old paint drum prior to it being returned to its correct container. The containers were wooden boxes and these lined the walls from floor to the rafters; there was no ceiling. For reasons known only to James, a square of old paper was placed into another drum each and every time that he placed a restored item in one of the drums.

Idle hands and all that . . . well, at slack times, when there were no ships in any of the drydocks, the apprentices would go looking for some diversion, and baiting James was a favoured pastime. You could always depend on James to liven things up and the best and surest way of achieving this was quite simple: just upset his paper drum, first being sure of a good clear exit, otherwise you could end up as dead meat on the Rivet Store floor. James never aimed to take prisoners: "kill the bastards" was his motto.

The Rivet Store was part of long timber building under a slate roof and adjacent on one side to the Shipwright's shop. Because there were no ceilings in any of the sections of this building, one could go from end to end whilst up in the rafters. James kept his door firmly locked. When he did open up, it was only the top half that unlocked, the bottom half was only opened to the Foreman or someone of similar status.

One of the more agile apprentices would get into the rafters and move along to a position above the Rivet Store and wait for developments. Another apprentice would go to the door of the Store and rattle to get James's attention, on the pretext of returning some item or other as instructed by his Foreman. Unless you made such a statement the door remained firmly locked.

When James moved to the door the lad above also moved. He, however, climbed down the front of the boxes which lined the walls at a point furthest away from James; no unnecessary risks were taken in this "game". Finally, when James had opened the top half door and was in conversation with the other apprentice, the lad inside the store collected the drum of paper pieces and returned as quickly as possible to the rafters.

The conversation broken off, James would close and lock the top half of the door and return to his work at his bench, whereupon he would realise that yet again he had fallen for the stupidity of the apprentices. His screams could be heard across the yard, and, as the crescendo peaked, you could be sure that the lad in the rafters had up-ended the paper drum so that pieces of paper fell like snowdrops on James.

Another method used to taunt James was rather more simple, though just as effective. When this was set up, the door of the Rivet Store would burst open and out he would charge, heading for the Shipwright's shop like a bull after the matador.

Two holes had been drilled in the wall which separated the Rivet Store from the Shipwright's Shop, at a point above James's work bench and directly in line with his vision. The person in the Shipwrights' Shop would push a piece of wooden dowling through one hole whilst shouting through the other hole "Shit".

This one shout could have an immediate or a delayed response, depending on the mood of James. The only certainty was that eventually the teasing would get to him, and then he would respond in the expected manner. On such occasions it was most unwise to be anywhere near the Rivet Store door when it flew open; indeed, to remain anywhere in that general area was courting disaster. James knew not who had been behind that partition, only that that it had been one of those stupid apprentices. Poor James, how he suffered.

The toilet facilities were of the dark ages and used only in a dire emergency; certainly one never loitered there, as is the custom in many of today's modern factory toilet blocks. Did you have to use them, it was a quick in and out. For my part I never used them at any time during my five-year stint.

The urinal was, I suppose, standard for the time, you "pointed Percy at the porcelain", this in company with every other visitor who had entered for that purpose. The "porcelain" was an open length of sewering, perhaps twenty feet long, fixed to one wall. The braggart, when he had a captive audience, would comment that the porcelain was cold on Percy, big lad.

The difference in the toilets at the Dockyard was in the "Shitshop". Whereas in other establishments these would be cubicles with some manner of privacy – albeit that this, in some I have seen, consisted only of a half door – the Dockyard did not have any such luxury. As with the urinal, this was an open length of sewer pipe, larger in diameter of course, and communal.

The open sewer pipe ran the length of one wall and fixed to the top of this was a length of timber into which had been cut holes of standard "bum" diameter. There were perhaps ten such holes, each divided from its neighbouring hole by a timber partitioning the width of the seating and perhaps two feet high. They were private only in the sense that you could not see your neighbour's bare bum. In all other regards it was definitely togetherness.

The flushing arrangement was automatic in that, when the tank positioned above the first trap was full, it released perhaps twenty gallons of water which then sped along the sewer pipe and under the bums of those perched on the seating, removing whatever needed to be removed. The flushing arrangement could be activated before the water had reached the automatic tip level simply by attaching a string to the release mechanism and pulling it, as and when required.

The reader is probably already ahead of me and can imagine that this arrangement was ripe for "fun". I can recall two types of prank which were in regular use, particularly with those who were unaware that anyone would stoop to such depths.

One such prank was the "hot arse" treatment and required that the top trap under the water tank was occupied by one of the gang who intended to "lift the bums". An accomplice would be in the vicinity of the entrance waiting for some likely candidate to arrive and head for the crap department. When he was certain that the victim was indeed heading in this direction he would commence to whistle some prearranged tune. Regardless of where the victim sat along the plank, he was about to have his arse scorched. The lad in the end trap lit a gradely ball of cotton waste which had been soaked in coal tar oil, this whilst he tripped the flush mechanism. When the torrent of water was past its first mad flush, he would lower the ball of ignited waste into the pipe so that it would sail under the unsuspecting "customers" perched along the length of the plank.

As the lad lowered the ball of waste, he stood up and departed by the door immediately to his right and was outside the premises before the waste "lit up" the first bum. All hell would then break out when men would be jumping up off the plank to ensure that they did not ruin their marriage prospects, all were of one mind threatening to kill whoever was responsible. However, seldom if ever did they know who had been in the end trap when they had entered because, for whatever reason, one never paid attention to those sitting along the plank.

Another prank was to take an oiler's brush, with a handle of perhaps two feet, into the crap department with you, together with your small tin of thick cylinder oil. Both items were secreted about your person and this, of course, required that you must sit next to the chosen victim.

When the victim was seated and doing that for which he had entered, the brush man would slip into the adjacent trap and immediately set about getting the brush out and giving the bristles a thorough coating of oil. When the brush was dripping with oil he would reach down the hole and proceed to paint the arse of the victim in the next trap. If the victim was not a very popular person it was not unknown for him to be held firmly to the seat by an accomplice to ensure that he was fully oiled.

Primitive as this toilet arrangement undoubtedly was, it was not a one-off nor exclusive to Dublin. An identical facility was in daily use at the Manchester Ship Canal repair yard at Ellesmere Port as late as 1958.

Word was circulated that a welder working in the Plating Shop was ripe for picking. He was not a very popular person and it was felt that it was time for him to be brought down a peg or three.

The man in question was welding seams along a length of plating which was clamped to the steel block flooring. Each seam was perhaps fifteen feet long and the welder was squatting, or rather crouching down, and working along the seam. His feet were either side of the weld area and as he squatted down his testicles dropped out through a split in his trousers; this, then was the target area.

A tin containing warmed cylinder oil (the warming was necessary to thin the oil, which was very thick) was attached to a length of timber, a man-helper, as used by painters to paint ship sides. The welder was a fiery character, very quick with his fists, so it was important that all exits were free and fully open.

The length of weld was such that the welder, when at the end of the run, was pretty close to a large shears/punching machine; certainly he was within reach of the man-helper and the tin of oil and most importantly, he had his back to the shears.

When he arrived at the required position, the lad with the tin of oil pushed the man-helper out along the seam beneath the welder and quickly departed the area. As the welding rod became shorter the welder squatted further down until the inevitable happened. Engrossed as he was in his work, and because the oil had been warmed, he did not realise that his testicles were well and truly in the thick of it.

The first indication that all was not well was when he straightened his knees, which action returned his oil-coated testicles to their rightful position. Even then I don't think that he really grasped the situation. He put his hand down to scratch himself and got a handful of oil, he knew then all right and really did not know how to tackle the situation.

Everyone around was doubled up laughing because by the time that he actually dunked his tatties a crowd had gathered. Who was responsible? Who would help him? Who should he strangle? He was beaten and he knew it so he gathered his composure and made off for the ''Shitshop'' to attempt to clean himself. Anyone who knows anything about cylinder oil will appreciate that

85

such cleaning was most difficult, even with warm soapy water which was not available in the Dockyard; so at best the victim could wipe off the excess.

Quite a number of Scots worked at the Dockyard, indeed some of the Foremen were Scots, due, I suppose, to the fact that a Scot had established the yard in the first place. I was party to an incident one day which involved two Scots, one of whom was a Foreman.

The Foreman had searched everywhere for this man, his fellow Scot, and when he eventually located him he rather heatedly enquired where he had been.

The man replied that he had been, as he put it, "For a shite"; the Foreman, not happy with this response, informed the man that he should shit in his own time. Quick as a flash back came the reply, "I make it in your time so I will drop it in your time". There was no answer to that, the Foreman turned on his heels and stormed away, forgetting that he wanted the man for something or other.

There was no time clock as we know it today, there was a Time Snatcher. This man sat at an open window of the Main Office and entering the yard you handed him a Time Sheet which indicated your hours for the previous day, and the ship upon which you had worked.

The Time Snatcher knew everyone, and could see everyone who passed, and of course did you not submit a Time Sheet then you were not paid, a simple but effective way of ensuring that you were on time. The office window was open for the minimum of time consistent with the number of employees expected for a particular day and as they entered the Time Snatcher gave each person a blank Time Sheet.

There were no tea breaks; drinking tea when you were paid to work was forbidden. As always the men did brew up when they could – correction, the tradesmen would instruct the apprentices to go and make a can of tea. There were no facilities for heating water unless there happened to be a Burner or other employee using oxy-acetylene equipment close by. Failing that, it was a question of dodging authority and making your way to the Blacksmith's Shop.

Getting to the Blacksmith's Shop was not always easy, and at unofficial tea breaks there was usually a queue in that area. One particular Blacksmith, nicknamed Tojo because of his likeness to the Japanese Premier, was always helpful. Indeed, on occasion he even went as far as having a second fire lit and available for the many tea cans that would require to be heated.

The procedure was to suspend the can of cold water over the blazing fire until it boiled, when the dry tea would be added. It was then held over the fire for a further period to ensure that it had been properly "wetted". You then ran back to your job area again, making sure that you did not encounter any Foreman or other authority.

Were you caught you would be made to empty the tea away. Yes, it may appear strange now, but that was the way of things then; everyone knew and accepted that this was what happened. You were paid to work, not to drink tea. When you were drinking tea you were robbing the boss, off the job, and *en route* to or from the Blacksmiths Shop to brew tea was far worse. We knew the penalty that would be exacted so we could not complain unless we were looking for another employer.

Difficult as it may be to accept, smoking was not allowed either, for again, if you were smoking, then you could not be using both hands for your employer. He paid your wages for the *whole* you; both hands were required when packing valves, caulking, riveting, whatever; when smoking you could not work efficiently and therefore you were cheating your employer.

The Managing Director was a big, imposing man who walked around and through every area of the yard each morning, this before he entered the offices. Whilst doing his rounds he nodded to his employees and if he spoke or addressed anyone it was only by surname. Grown men would quickly dispose of their cigarettes and waft away all traces of smoke when they knew that he was nearby. When he was in an area everyone gave of their best, this even if doing nothing. The Managing Director was held in awe; his imposing appearance, apart from the fact that he had so much power over the lives of the employees, was sufficient to ensure that he was indeed the all powerful.

There were two Dockyards in Dublin in those days and, as the bulk of the labour floated between these two establishments, it was essential that your work record was good at both. Were it not, then you might as well forget about ship repair work as a means of earning a living. As far as labour was concerned, the two yards had a close liaison, essential to maintain the strangle hold they enjoyed over the men's lives.

One Foreman, if summoned to the office, would immediately remove his cap and rub its dirty external surface across his face to ensure that on entering the office he gave the right impression, a hard-working Supervisor was most definitely a "hands-on person"; were he clean of hands and attire, then he was not at the sharp end of the activity and really not fully aware of what his men were doing.

The outside Manager was of the same ilk. He did not manage from a distance but got right down to the job to ensure that it was being carried out correctly. He carried a small brown case which, in addition to holding his necessary papers, also held a boilersuit which he donned as and when necessary. I have seen him crawl into the furnace of a boiler and wriggle along its length to enter the combustion chamber and inspect the progress of the job in hand.

Everyone earned their corn in those days from the Manager downwards. A Supervisor, Manager or simply Chargehand had the capability to undertake each and every facet of any job that was within his sphere of responsibility. Did you encounter any difficulty with a job, you could rely on the Supervisor to show you how to solve the problem and for this they had your greatest respect. They were true craftsmen who had earned their stripes because of their professionalism; nepotism, drinking at the same pub or sharing a similar hobby as the boss were never enough to ensure promotion; job knowledge was the sole criterion.

In 1945 the working week was forty-eight hours, this through five and a half days ending at noon each Saturday. Wages were paid at the final hour and collected as you departed the premises through the Main Entrance. It was not unusual to see a man's wife waiting outside the gates to intercept her husband before he made off to the nearest pub with his wages. She wanted her share so that she could purchase food for the weekend, and, in some instances, to attend the local Pawn Shop and redeem the husband's one and only suit and her best dress. These were essential for Mass the following morning.

The only exception to this method of payment was when the men would be laid off, then pay day could be any day. The pay packet was a sealed brown envelope and the wage detail was written on the front, rate per hour, number of hours worked, etc. Deductions were few, a Hospital Levy of twopence, this for regular employees only; Income Tax was not deducted but was the responsibility of each person on an annual basis.

Chapter Eleven

During my time at the Dockyard, I worked on two ships which foundered shortly after leaving the yard. Their loss, however, was no reflection on the quality of workmanship. One vessel, the M.V. *Albany*, was lost with all hands off the coast of Wales whilst in ballast on a passage from Wexford to Port Talbot. She entered the yard as the *Empire Albany*, having recently been purchased by her owner and master Captain Dowd. The *Empire* was deleted from her name during her time in the yard, but only on her bow and stern; the lifeboats, etc., remained unchanged.

When the *Albany* foundered the first indication that she had been lost was when a lifeboat was discovered and, as the name had not been changed, she was incorrectly reported lost as the *Empire Albany*. In fact, this detail was on the records of the Lowestoft Ship Society as late as the seventies; this I discovered in an article in *Sea Breezes*. I wrote to the Society indicating what I knew about the incident, pointing out that the *Empire* part of her name had been deleted prior to her departure from the Ringsland Dockyard.

The other vessel was the three-masted schooner *Isallt* which was forced onto a sand-bank off the coast at Ballymoney, Co. Wexford, on Thursday 4th December 1947 during a severe storm. There were but two survivors. The *Isallt* was typical of many such vessels which plied the Irish sea at that time, and were regular visitors to the Dockyard.

Built at Porthmadoc in 1909, she was rigged as a topsail schooner, her headsails set on a jib-boom and bowsprit complete with martingale, bobstays and dolphin striker. She was a workhorse that had survived many stormy and difficult passages not only on the Irish Sea but across the North Atlantic and even to South America for hides, which she would take into Runcorn, Cheshire, for use in the local tanning industry.

The thing that struck me about this vessel more than any other that I recall was her master, Captain Charles McGuinness. After the *Isallt* went out of the yard she lay at an adjacent dock and Captain McGuinness passed through the yard almost every day, a striking person, at least that is how I remember him. After his death it transpired that he had been a most exceptional person who amongst his achievements had been navigator when Admiral Byrd explored the South Pole. At other times during his life he had been a soldier, gun runner, rum runner, pearl diver, guerilla fighter and explorer. All this is detailed in his book *Sailor of Fortune* published in 1935.

When working outside the Dockyard on some vessel that was working cargo along the quays, in particular the North Wall area, we used the Dublin Corporation ferries which plied the river: Ringsend Point – Tobins Corner – North Wall.

The ferry charge of one penny was paid by the Dockyard by way of a voucher which resembled the old-fashioned bus/tram tickets. When instructed to attend some ship which required that you used the ferry, you went into the office and were issued with the necessary tickets. The ferry was manned by two people, a lad who collected the fares, and the Captain/Driver.

Early mornings, when the ferry was crowded with dockers, we used to try and dodge parting with the penny ticket, moving along the ferry from port to starboard as the lad came along collecting fares. On some occasions, this depending on the weather and the location of the ship relative to Butt Bridge, we would use our bicycles to get to the job.

In each case the aim was to amass some ferry tickets and to convert these to ready cash. This we achieved with the assistance of one particular ferry lad who, being on very low wages, was not adverse to closing his eyes to our dodging him and not offering our tickets.

The system was as follows; the lad paid us a halfpenny for each penny ticket that we gave him. Tickets were not returned to the Dockyard by the Corporation at regular intervals but taken to the Dockyard office by the ferry lads at slack times through the day when it was possible for the ferry to run with one person. We each made a halfpenny per ticket and, if you were out all week along the quays, it was possible to enhance your pocket money by a full threepence, old money, and at 2.4 to the current penny the income would not be as Arthur Daly would say, "A nice little earner". Still, for a first-year apprentice it would equate with the pay for two hours' work.

One ferry Driver earned himself the nick name of "Old lashed-to-the helm", this because of his reluctance to cross the river at the slightest sign of a breeze. It did on occasion get a little rough at this crossing point, although nothing to cause concern to anyone excepting this particular ferryman, and when he did decide that he was not going to sail despite a crowd waiting to cross, he was called some terrible names.

Dockers working the colliers were required in those days to supply their own shovels; long-handled, with a heart-shaped spade end, they were good weapons and there were times when "Old lashed-to-the-helm" was told to cast off or have his head caved in. Some choice. However, when the result of crossing or not crossing the river was food or no food, one could understand the dockers' annoyance.

There was no canteen at the Dockyard. Those men who did not live locally, and therefore could not go home, simply sat about at the back of machinery or wherever and ate their sandwiches. Neither was there any washing facility other than a bucket of cold water, usually with a thick scum due to the number of people who had used it. On really cold freezing days, and if there was an oxyacetylene set handy, a piece of iron bar would be heated until it was red hot at which time it was dropped into the bucket to heat the water.

There were some radical changes in 1948–1949 which really brought us into the twentieth century. Earth shattering – the men could hardly believe what was happening. The "Shitshop" was modernised, out went the communal crappery to be replaced with cubicles which had FULL doors which could be bolted. This change saw men who hitherto would not go within twenty feet of the toilets wishing for a bout of diarrhoea just to get into the place and enjoy the new comforts. The greatest change was that a disused room beneath the Drawing Office was transformed and converted into a Rest Room with tables, seating and a stove. . . . Yes, the dark ages were over, the men could sit down and eat their lunch like human beings instead of being huddled up behind some machine.

There was a catch, however, and one wonders whether or not this "canteen" had really been set up to be of benefit to the employees. It was located directly opposite the Time Snatcher's office and afforded him a grandstand view of the comings and goings of the men. He could see them start and finish their lunch break; they were as the goldfish, always under the eye. The men soon recognised that this facility, although welcomed and long overdue, had not been created for their comfort but was established so that a better check could be maintained on their movements. It was not too long before the building was returned to its disused state.

Every apprentice who entered the Dockyard had to spend a period of time in the Blacksmith's Shop. If memory serves me right, the duration was usually about three months. Some of the work in that area was most interesting. In particular I recall that I enjoyed assisting with fire welding when three people were required, two to hold the item to be welded – the Blacksmith and the extra person – and the striker to hammer the joint closed. The striker's hammer weighed perhaps seven pounds and he would swing this up and down at a rapid rate to strike the point indicated by the Blacksmith's small hammer. This was really fascinating work to watch and speed was essential if the weld was to be successful.

The worst job in that area was breaking coke for the fires, very hard work which everyone dreaded. The coke had to be broken down to particles of about half-inch diameter, then it was riddled to remove the dust, bagged and brought indoors.

If the men were asked to work overtime to complete some job for which there was an urgent requirement (this was the only occasion when overtime was worked), it was accepted that they would have a cup of tea. No official rest period, simply a grudging acceptance of the men's need for a cup of tea and perhaps a bite to eat.

The senior apprentice lived in hope that, whatever the job, it would take hours to complete, in which case the men would most definitely want something to eat. Obtaining the required food, going around the men and taking their orders and their money, was his jealously guarded "perk". When he had completed his rounds he would then seek out the junior apprentice and despatch him to the local shop to collect the "goodies".

Now, as far as the senior apprentice was concerned all the men wanted a slice of "Wet Nellie". Some may have wanted a change but he would endeavour to get them to alter their thinking. Some he won, some he lost; whichever way the penny fell, you could be sure that the bulk of the order was for "Wet Nellie".

Wet Nellie was a concoction which comprised the scrapings of the Bakery work tables, all mixed together and baked on trays to produce a slab roughly four foot by two, and about two inches thick. After removal from the oven, and when it had cooled slightly, the top was coated with a pink icing. The wonders which lay beneath the pink covering, and the rubbish, had to be experienced. No two days were the same; some days it was good, another – well, the coating was constant and what the hell? It filled a hole.

FAREWELL, DUBLIN, BUT NEVER GOODBYE

A slice of "Wet Nellie" measured four inches by four and cost threepence. Some days it was as light as a feather, another it was like lead. When you returned to the Dockyard you took the order to the senior apprentice, never to the men, not even when we knew who had ordered what. The senior apprentice was in charge of distribution, and as stated he had to have his little "perk".

When he received the "goodies" he opened the bags, removed each piece of "Wet Nellie" which he then proceeded to reduce in size to three inches by three. The results of this cutting was that he gained seven square inches of "Wet Nellie" for each portion purchased, not quite the sixty/forty split that he would have liked but it was sufficient and, most important, the men were satisfied and always considered that they had received good value.

The senior apprentice distributed the off-cuts as he saw fit, which usually meant that the most junior apprentice seldom if ever got any. Never mind, that was the way of things and, of course, we knew that our day would come: your apprenticeship was much like the rungs of a ladder, the higher you went the more you could see and, all being well, the more you could have.

Sadly, however, by the time that I was senior apprentice the place was in decline, this in some measure due to the strengthening of the Union's hold over Management. The Unions had little or no power in 1945, however this situation had dramatically changed by 1950 and much of the "Hire and Fire" that had existed was now a thing of the past.

Whereas there had been very few regular employees other than apprentices in the period 1945–1950, the Union sought to change this and negotiated a deal to reduce the apprentice ratio to one to every four tradesmen. The thinking here was that if there were fewer apprentices then the Dockyard would be required to carry a larger number of regular tradesmen. This to ensure that they had the capability to attend to any urgent work which might be on offer rather than carry on with the old situation where they contracted for work; then, when they had secured a contract, they would seek the necessary labour to complete the task.

Sound thinking. However, in the long term the losers, as ever, were the men because the regular work force was not increased. There was, indeed, a reduction in the number of trainees employed to the ratio suggested by the Unions. In real terms nothing changed; the regular weekly wage bill was considerably reduced which situation pleased the owner.

There was much talk of trying to make the yard a closed shop. Indeed, it was suggested that all apprentices should join the Union. All this was just talk, it

93

was recognised by the more enlightened that any positive move in that direction would result in immediate closure.

Still, the seed had been planted and unrest was evident, in particular apprentices in the Shipwright area appeared to be most active and it was clear that they were being closely observed to see how much support was forthcoming from other apprentices.

We eventually joined the Union but, it should be said, under duress, as many did not really want to get involved as it was thought that, should the situation deteriorate when the men were called out on strike, the owner might terminate the apprenticeship of any youngster who went out with the men.

In the end the hot-heads won the day and a strike was called, this perhaps two weeks before we were to experience some atrocious weather and when there was little or no work in the yard. The timing could not have been worse.

We were told to remain at work, the men were on picket duty outside the gates and daily they would interrogate passing apprentices to impress on them that they MUST not do men's work. Naturally we said, "No way"; however, inside it was quite different and we got on with whatever job we were given with little or no concern for those outside. The weather deteriorated, there was ice everywhere and conditions in the unheated workshops were really very bad. The only warm place was in the Blacksmith's Shop and whenever possible we would make our way there to defrost.

The apprentices in the Shipwright Shop were told to prepare the main dry-dock for a ship, a Board of Works dredger, which was lying across the Grand Canal Basin from the yard. These lads were most vocal in terms of supporting the men outside. They argued about all and every job: "That's men's work" was their daily gripe. It came therefore as no surprise when we were informed that they had refused to prepare the graving dock as instructed.

Vantage observation points were manned by the other apprentices so that we were fully informed of developments. The Foreman had gone to the main office to report that the lads had refused to follow instructions; the entire yard was buzzing, this was the test case for all. If these lads got away with their refusal then those on strike would insist that the other apprentices follow their example.

We did not have to wait very long for the answer. The Foreman returned and told the lads that either they did as they were told or went up the yard to have their apprenticeships terminated. Hard times, hard words – they were given no time to consider, it was an immediate "take it or leave it" situation with no bargaining: do it now or put on your coat and go home.

Some apprentices decided that in fairness to the men they should depart, this in the belief that the ultimate price would not be extracted. They were very wrong; they went up the road and stayed there, never to come through the gates again.

The unrest was quelled, the lads had made a brave stand and they had achieved nothing except the loss of their jobs. In these circumstances, therefore, it was not surprising that the other lads around the yard quickly put their heads down and got on with whatever work they were given, be this men's work or otherwise, and to be perfectly honest everything we did *was* men's work.

The rebels who remained prepared the graving dock as instructed and, come the day that the dredger was to enter the dock, they really sampled the bottom of the barrel. Management did not take kindly to being put on the rack. They had the upper hand now and they were going to demonstrate for all to see that they would tolerate no dissent, particularly not from lads whom they had taken out of the gutter.

We watched from afar lest it be thought that we supported their actions. As stated, the dredger was lying across the Basin from the Dockyard, a distance of some 300 m and she had no power; the passage across would be by use of her winches and ropes and the apprentices' muscle power.

The weather was at its worst, the water of the Basin was all but frozen. The work which was about to begin would, under normal circumstances, have been carried out by casual labour on a job and finish basis.

Things weren't normal, though; *the* owner had many lads who had to be shown just who was boss – why employ others when the lads were available and willing? They must have been willing, otherwise they would have departed with the hot-heads, was the reasoning, so the order was given that the apprentices should rig the necessary blocks, etc., along and across the Canal Basin, so that by using the dredger's hand-winches she could be pulled across and into the graving dock.

Although it was freezing cold the lads soon had a sweat on. There was no let-up, no tea nor lunch break, just hard work until late that afternoon when the ship was positioned central in the graving dock. They were then sent home and told to return early the following morning when the dock would be pumped dry.

The strike was broken shortly after this as first one and then another of the tradesmen drifted back to work. Nothing had been gained other than an agreement by the owner to employ fewer apprentices, a situation which he considered most acceptable. As far as he was concerned, those who remained would just have to work that much harder, and I can assure you that they did.

Little wonder then that the words "SLAVE LABOUR" had been painted on the Dockyard perimeter wall. Every wage paid was the very minimum acceptable to the workers, there were no extras other than a further helping of graft and, were you unhappy with that, then you had a choice – go up the road.

During my five-year stint I pondered many times as to why men allowed themselves to be treated in such an uncaring manner. They counted as nothing were they not toiling every minute of every day, at times in conditions which no words of mine could adequately describe.

However, at that time there was no alternative; it was Hobson's Choice, give of your all and afford your family some little dignity, or gain the reputation of being a trouble-maker and never work in either of the two ship repair yards that existed in Dublin at that time. Not surprisingly, therefore, the men endured the severe hardships which were part and parcel of working at the Ringsend Dockyard; half a crust was better than none and, what the Hell, was not all life hard? A yoke there was little different from one elsewhere, so they soldiered on and grew old early, if at all.

The adage "Die young and have a good-looking corpse" was not applicable here, for the young were old before their time and the old were dead, or at best close to it.

Chapter Twelve

That, then, was the Dublin that I departed all those years ago. Whilst I was happy to be going, my mother was crying her eyes out and praying that the good Lord up there in the Heavens would put his foot out and kick some sense into me. ''What would your father think?'' she kept repeating like a cracked record. What indeed, thought I, him having been dead for two years.

It was not as if I was happy at the thoughts of leaving home and having to totally fend for myself – that part did bother me. However, I was determined to join the Merchant Service and that required that I leave home. You can't take the family with you, they must stop and you must go; so it was that I got into a relation's car for the trip to the North Wall and the B & I. ferry to Liverpool.

Arriving at Liverpool I had no idea of how to go about getting a ship. No forward planning for this lad – only get to Liverpool, there are plenty of ships there.

Upon arrival in Liverpool, I was only sure of one thing, this was that my chance of getting a ship on my first day was very remote. My first concern must be accommodation and this, if at all possible, at some Sailor's Home, I would be closer to the action, to people who knew the ropes who could direct me in my search. During my time at the Rita Mooney School of Acting I had sung many times at the Apostleship of the Sea, so that is where I made for. If a small city like Dublin had such a place, unquestionably Liverpool would have a large one.

Sure enough there was one, and this not too far from Lime Street Station whence I had made my way from the ferry. Following the directions given, I soon arrived there and was more than pleased to learn that, yes, they did have a room available, and that the price per night for bed and breakfast was seven shillings and sixpence (thirty-seven and a half new pence). Other meals you bought as and when you wanted at the usual meal times.

Having settled in, I returned to the Reception desk to enquire how to go about achieving my ambition. The resident Priest, an Irishman, was most helpful. He knew precisely what had to be done; I must sign on at the Federation of Ship Owners (The Seaman's Pool), Officer Department, where arrangements would be made for me to attend for grading. At that time all aspiring ship's engineers had to be graded; time-served Dockyard apprentices, with some examinations successfully passed, obtained the higher gradings and usually would obtain a position in preference to another lower-graded applicant.

By noon on day one I had been graded, passed the required medical examination and was in possession of my Discharge Book. I returned to my temporary home well satisfied with the morning's work and sat down to my first proper meal since leaving home.

I had been told to report back to the Federation at 2.30 p.m. when I might be in line for an interview with a Shipping Agent who was acting for a London ship owner.

The appointed time saw me first in line at the Federation Office, I was anxious and it showed. I had indicated during my initial visit that regular trade was not for me; New York to Liverpool on a schedule liner service did not appeal. My ambition was to see the world, not two ports every couple of weeks. I was after a mystery tour, sailing away to wherever to tramp the seven seas; a cargo here, there, any which where – duration, who cares? Just let me get away on the ocean wide. There were no ties, so who was worried about getting back.

Yes, the Federation had arranged for an interview, I should attend the address given at 3.30 p.m. when I would be assessed for suitability as fifth Engineering Officer for the S.S. *Kingsmount* which would dock at Hamburg in five days' time. The man behind the desk gave me instructions on how to get to the office of the Shipping Agent and wished me luck. Whatever the result I must, the man informed me, return to the Federation Office the following morning.

The interview, which I had expected to be pretty thorough and which caused palpitations when I located and entered the Agent's office, was a nothing affair. The man who interviewed me knew that this would be my first ship; he also knew the details of my grading and that I was the product of a Dockyard, so I would therefore have some knowledge of ships.

After a few very basic questions the man stated that I was engaged as fifth engineer for the S.S. *Kingsmount* which was bound for Hamburg from America and due to arrive there in five days' time. The rate of pay would be £26 per month, to commence when Articles were signed at the Federation Offices in two days' time. An advance of pay would also be available, if required, at that time. I thanked the man and came out of the office on cloud nine. I wanted to tell everyone about my good fortune, so that they could share in my euphoria.

Back at the Apostleship of the Sea, I told all and sundry; anyone who would listen got the full details. Anyone would think that I was the first person ever to join a ship. Looking back, I am sure that I was a complete and utter bore, I completely overlooked the fact that each resident was himself a seaman who was either on leave from his ship, or, as I learned later, studying in readiness for sitting for one of his "Tickets" – all seasoned deep-sea men who had heard ducks fart before. They were very nice and wished me good luck, some adding that I should keep my head down and study at every opportunity.

Come the appointed day I was first in the queue at the Shipping Office when the Ship's Articles were read to the seamen who had been selected as crew members for the S.S. *Kingsmount en route* America to Hamburg. The procedure was quite alien to me, for I had no idea of what was happening other than that I had been told to attend for the signing of Articles.

The man in the Shipping Office had said that I should just listen and step forward when the position of fifth Engineer was called, at which time I was to tender my Discharge Book to the Shipping Superintendent at the desk. He also informed me that the Engineers would sign on in order of rank, Chief Engineer first, followed by the Second Engineer, etc., each in turn signing the Ship's Articles as offered by the ship's Captain. Also signed was an Allotment Note for £10 per month which money would be sent by the Shipping Company directly to my mother. This level of wage division in support of the family unit was maintained until I married when, with a home of my own to support, my finances had to be re-assessed.

So it was that I signed on my first ship in Liverpool and, as advised by the Shipping Office official, I gathered with the other Engineers after the signing of Articles when the Chief Engineer invited us to join him for drinks. We were the most multinational gathering of Engineers I was ever to sail with: English, Irish, Scottish and Polish.

During the course of drinks we introduced ourselves, giving a brief history of past ships and in particular what, if any, knowledge anyone had of Canadian "Fort" boats. It had been established that the *Kingsmount* was a Canadian Fort-Type Ship which had been built in Canada during the Second World War. Opinions were mixed as to the quality of these ships, one of the assembled Engineers adding that, as they had been built in a hurry, they were not very dependable. Poor workmanship throughout, according to the Scottish Second Engineer who not surprisingly voiced the opinion that a Clyde-built ship was the only proper ship afloat.

Years later, I was to discover that the S.S. *Kingsmount* had been built by West Coast Shipbuilders Ltd., Vancouver, B.C., and laid down as the Kootenay Park in August 1942. During building her name was changed and she was eventually launched as the *Fort Carlton*. In October 1944 she was renamed *Fort Nisqually* and, coming under the Red Ensign in 1950, she was renamed *Kingsmount*, one of two ships owned by the Capeside Steamship Co.

She remained as the *Kingsmount* until 1957, at which time she had a further name change and, as the *Monteplata* she sailed until 1961, when she changed names again to become the *Ekila*. The last known information is that she became the *Loyal Fortunes* in 1965. Clearly she had many owners and one wonders why; was she a bogey ship which never really paid her way with any owner? One of those ships which was forever a problem and always costing her owner money? Certainly she was a problem when I sailed in her, and in seven months' sailing she only managed to pick up and discharge two successful cargoes, the last of which was a straight run, from North Africa to Rotterdam for major repairs.

A full crew departed Liverpool to join the *Kingsmount* at Hamburg, leaving one cold wintry morning by train for London and Dover to catch the night ferry to Ostend; then on by train to Hamburg, where a coach was laid on to take us to a small lighter which landed us on a coal wharf astern of the ship.

I rather doubt that any of us expected the sight which was to greet us that cold afternoon. When the *Kingsmount* came within our field of vision we could not believe our eyes. Certainly she was the dirtiest ship that I had ever seen – no clean lines here, just a rust tub which set everyone wondering what her interior must be like. Some suggested that she had just had a rough passage across the North Atlantic and she would be as pretty as a picture within; wrong, wrong, she was just as bad within and I doubt that there was one amongst us who did not regret joining her.

There was a scratch crew aboard to welcome us and, after we had sorted our belongings to our cabins, the Engineers mustered in the smoke room where a drunken Irishman held forth. It was eventually established that he was the departing Chief Engineer and, apart from a German Donkeyman on temporary engagement, he was the only remaining member of the previous engine room staff.

Discharge was almost complete and we were informed that the ship would sail the following morning, so watches had to be set more or less straight away. The Second Engineer went aft to the Firemen's and Greasers' quarters to inform them of the situation and to sort out watches with the Donkeyman, at which time it was discovered that two Firemen had failed to join the party at Liverpool the previous morning. Why it had taken until then to establish this fact was beyond me. Surely the Captain should have undertaken a roll call at Lime Street station, when the Chief Engineer would have been forewarned that he would not have a full complement to man the engine room.

The first and most important task which faced the Engineers was the taking aboard of bunkers, fuel oil and fresh water, as necessary for the boilers to generate steam with which to power the ship. Whilst the other Engineers set about this task, I was detailed to check aboard and arrange storage for the essential replacement stores which had been ordered by the previous Chief Engineer.

In this connection the Second Engineer simply gave me a detailed list as passed along by the departing inebriated Chief Engineer; "Check these items aboard and get the Donkeyman to store them away." Although I was a product of a Dockyard, with a reasonable knowledge of ships, there was much to learn in terms ship's stores and as a consequence most of that which had come aboard simply went below unchecked – this simply because I was not familiar with many items. The task was such that it was not completed until the following day, by which time we were sailing towards the English Channel.

I was instructed to join the Second Engineer on the four to eight watch as soon as the stores were below deck, I was to be his assistant, when I would learn how everything worked. I was very naive in those days, thinking that nights were made for sleeping. Four to eight seemed reasonable to me; four hours' work each day, OK, so it was a late finish but I would get used to that.

Clearly there were two periods of four to eight in each twenty-four hours and I was expected to be in the engine room for each. It was almost the death of me. By the third day I was in a trance. I came off watch, went straight to my cabin and promptly fell asleep on my couch. On day three, when I had not been seen in the lounge for a meal, the Chief came to my cabin, woke me and said, "Son, if you don't get a grip on yourself you will crack up." Then he explained that I must pace myself to get used to the idea of sleeping in two bits – 9.00 p.m. until 3.30 a.m., and then again after lunch, 1.30 until 3.30, gave me a total of eight and a half hours in my bed every twenty-four hours, a figure which I agreed was more than I had been getting at home every weekend. Eventually, like all seafarers, I was to become quite used to a broken sleep pattern. There was an old adage about sleep in those days; the requirement was as follows, six hours for a man, seven for a woman, and eight for a fool.

We were in ballast for America and sailing like an empty biscuit tin, high in the water and rolling until at times I wondered if we should ever recover. The first hint of what was to come occurred when we were in the Bay of Biscay in heavy seas. The fan engine, which produced the forced draught necessary for the oil-fired boilers, broke down, and we were all called to the engine room to help effect repairs.

Eventually the fault was rectified and we returned to a normal shift pattern. All went well for about four hours. Then further problems forced us to make for the port of Horta in the Azores Islands, where more lasting repairs would be undertaken.

Sailing again we ran into the mother and father of a storm, when it was discovered that the mechanism which automatically cut the steam to the main engine when the propeller came out of the water, had malfunctioned. As a consequence of this the engine was shaking itself to bits; whereas the normal engine revolutions were sixty-five rpm, these were increasing to ninety plus as the ship dipped her bow into the sea, at which time her stern lifted high in the air, freeing the propeller from the water. The answer to this problem was to operate the mechanism manually.

Watches were doubled to provide two Engineers per watch and thereby allow for one to control the steam cut-off lever. This required an Engineer to sit adjacent to the cut-off lever and to operate same to instantly stop the flow of steam to the engine when he sensed that the stern was rising, at which time the water pressure on the propeller would decrease thereby allowing the engine to race. The cut-off procedure was reversed when it was felt that the propeller was again fully submerged in the sea.

This was very taxing work and after an hour you felt as if your arms were dead. The ship's pitching did not help and I recall times when the effort necessary to maintain your position by the lever was such that you failed to cut the steam. At such times the engine raced at an incredible speed and was quite frightening to watch; falling back into the sea, the pressure almost stopped the engine turning.

At the height of the storm the fan engine again failed and nothing we could do would encourage it to function. The boilers were but onto natural draught, which required that the stokehold ventilators were kept "on the wind". However, this soon presented another problem in that we occasionally shipped a large sea down a ventilator. Turning the ventilators off the wind meant that we were not getting sufficient air to the fires, so proper combustion was not possible and as a consequence the fires were not burning efficiently.

All manner of innovations were attempted to maintain power and thereby ride out the storm. Eventually, after a couple of boiler blow backs when one of the firemen was seriously burned, the Chief Engineer told the Captain that he would have to stop the engines as to do otherwise could have serious consequences and possibly even result in death.

So it was that the engines were stopped and we started to transmit MAYDAY calls for assistance. The ship looked ready to call it a day, the pitching worsened to a degree when there were times when we all expected her to go under. The Captain asked that we try to get sufficient power to the engine to allow the ship to maintain her head to the storm. Again the boilers were flashed; this time, however, the lower half of the smokebox uptake doors were opened in an effort to increase the flow of air up the funnel, and thereby aid combustion.

We had some little success and managed to maintain headway. Soon, however, it was again necessary to shut down the engine, at which time all hands made their way to the bridge area of the ship to sit it out and await assistance.

Eventually our S.O.S. was answered and the Royal Navy frigate *Sparrow* radioed that she was on her way to us. Needless to say we were overjoyed and many eyes scanned the horizon for signs of a ship. When she was spotted a great cheer went up and you could sense that you had not been alone in being frightened.

Arriving on the scene in mountainous seas, the *Sparrow* proceeded to launch a lifeboat which headed towards us. One minute she was there in front of your eyes, the next she was out of sight, lost it appeared in some trough. Again the launch appeared, this time closer to us, until eventually she was in our lee, at which time three seamen managed to climb aboard.

Aboard came an Officer, a Signalman and another Rating, also a small line which was used to pull aboard a larger line. Larger and larger lines were drawn across until eventually we had a proper tow line attached; then the order was given to take up the slack and proceed to tow.

After five days the *Sparrow* brought us to safe harbour in St. George's, Bermuda. Minor repairs were effected there, sufficient to enable us to proceed to Hamilton, the capital of Bermuda, where the fan engine was fully repaired. The problem was one of spares; all we required was a set of piston rings but the owners had not thought these essential, so they were not stocked. Clearly a case of spoiling the ship for a pennyworth of tar.

At Hamilton, the ship's Agent informed the Captain that a couple of his seamen had ended up in the local jail, and that money was necessary to effect their release. The Captain elected to leave them where they were, stating that he would only arrange for their release come sailing day. In the meantime, to prevent any further problems, he refused to grant the crew any more money.

Whilst this radical step appeared to be the correct way to control the wayward crew, it was to backfire on the Officers. The morning following the Captain's edict, when the Officers gathered in the saloon for breakfast, it was discovered that there were neither table cloths nor cutlery and only a minimum of crockery. The crew, deprived of finances, had managed to raise cash by the simple expedient of selling ship's property ashore.

When this matter was resolved, we learned that the Captain had Logged those responsible several days' wages apiece. Logging, I was to learn, was at that time quite uncommon, a product of yesteryear, of the dark ages. Logging was a regular feature at every port throughout that trip; at "Pay Off" the Shipping Master commented that he had never known such level of Logging, to which the Captain replied that he had never in all his years at sea sailed with such a difficult crew.

Sailing from Bermuda we arrived at Norfolk, U.S.A. to pick up a cargo of coal for Japan, which instruction caused more trouble with some of the crew members who had been under the impression that they had signed Articles for a voyage of perhaps six weeks' duration, Hamburg – U.S.A. – England.

It then transpired that the Third Engineer had been given the same information in Liverpool and had planned to sit for his "Ticket" on the basis of that advice. Needless to say, there were many long faces and much discussion of how matters could be resolved.

For his part, the Captain simply quoted the Articles which clearly stated that the crew had signed "Foreign"; that is to say they had contracted for a minimum of two years, unless of course the ship was to dock in a U.K. port, in which eventuality Articles would be opened when the cargo was discharged. As it was, and regardless of what had been stated by the Shipping Office at Liverpool, a Contract had been offered and accepted, the crew must abide by it.

Sailing south from Norfolk heading for the Panama Canal, we again suffered problems in the engine room. This time it was boiler trouble, when two boiler tubes burst, which resulted in the shutting down of that particular boiler. The boiler was isolated and "Blown Down", that is the pressure was released into the sea through the ship's side.

When the pressure was zero all hands mustered to tackle the job of plugging the offending tubes. This required us to remove the superheater tubes and blank off the steam, after which it was relatively easy to insert special caps over the ruptured tubes, securing these in position with long one-inch diameter steel rods. When this work was completed steam was again raised, the three boilers "coupled" and the ship once more under full power.

Nearing Panama, further tubes ruptured and the boiler was again isolated and its pressure released. As we were close to Panama it was decided to continue the voyage on two boilers and to radio ahead and request the ship's Agent to contact the owners at London for permission to have the boiler retubed at Panama.

So it was that we spent approximately two weeks in the port of Cristobel/Colon, at the mouth of the Panama Canal straddling the U.S.A./Panama border. Whilst there I was to observe an innovation which I had never considered possible, in my book boilers produced steam pressure, which in turn was the motive power for all shipboard equipment.

Not on that occasion; high pressure air lines were brought aboard and these were used to pressurise the boilers. Ancillary machinery, domestic/sanitary water pumps and our generators were then operated on air rather than steam pressure, which innovation meant that the engine room, rather than being very hot, was relatively cool and a more pleasant place in which to undertake the vast number of jobs that required attention.

Again there were crew problems, with some members ending up in the local prison. They never appeared to learn – get into port, get drunk and start a fight was all they seemed to live for. It was all so alien to me; it was as if the ship's sole purpose was to transport them around the world, a drunken cruise on which work was a dirty word and something that others attended to.

The day came when the shore people had finished their work and steam had to be raised. This was a manual job, in that a hand pump was used to fire the boiler using a special light-weight oil. The manual effort necessary for this work would, under normal circumstances, be provided by the Firemen/Greasers, but not on that occasion. Knowing what was required of them, they had all done a runner ashore. Again the labour was provided by the Engineers.

Through the Panama Canal and up the West Coast of America to San Diego, where it was planned to take bunkers sufficient for the run across the Pacific Ocean to Japan. Upon arrival and after bunkering the Port Authorities would not clear us for sailing because we were too low in the water.

The problem was the result of our delay at Panama. We had loaded to the correct Plimsoll mark at Norfolk; however, the delay encountered *en route* was such that we were not in compliance with the Plimsoll requirement for crossing the Pacific at that time of year. Eventually, after a combination of reducing bunker oil and fresh water, and off-loading some cargo, we met the requirement and were cleared to sail.

Whilst the trip across the Pacific was uneventful, as was our discharge at the port of Muroran on Hokkaido, which is the most northern of the two islands which comprise Japan, thereafter further problems were to beset us. The ship was fated, nothing appeared to go to plan; as one problem was resolved, another, usually more serious, developed. It was crisis after crisis.

Our cargo was coal and having observed coal being discharged in Dublin by hand I was interested to see how others tackled this laborious work. The method of discharge at Muroran was almost identical, coal was loaded manually into half-ton tipping buckets and hoisted from the hold using the ship's equipment; the difference was that the dockers working our cargo, in the hold loading coal into buckets and driving the winches, were female, petite women who looked so out of place doing such work. The cargo, which was only worked during daylight hours, took sixteen days to unload.

In subsequent years, engaged in the coal trade from the east coast of America, Newport News or Norfolk in Virginia to the Continent, it is worth mentioning that we could load a full cargo under the tipplers at either port in approximately four hours; then, using large grabs, discharge at Rotterdam could be effected in about thirty-six hours.

We departed Japan with orders to proceed to China to load general cargo at several ports, *en route* the holds were to be thoroughly cleaned.

Our route south took us through the Sea of Japan, close to Korea where the Americans were at war, advice to all vessels sailing in those waters was to fly your National flag to facilitate identification by the many fighter planes in the skies at that time. The significance of this precaution was brought home one bright sunny afternoon, and a very frightening experience it was.

For my part, I can say in all honesty that what occurred almost caused a bowel evacuation; it was certainly more frightening than anything which occurred early on in the voyage, when we were adrift in the North Atlantic. Leaving the saloon after lunch one day, I proceeded aft to my cabin across the open deck, feeling well satisfied with myself that here I was seeing the world and being paid, fed and watered into the bargain. It was that sort of day – I'd just enjoyed a good meal and was strolling along a ship's deck in tropical conditions, at peace with everyone and everything.

When halfway across the open space I heard a shout, "Get down quick!" at the same time I heard the roar of aeroplanes approaching us very low and at high speed. There was nowhere to go; as it was I was rooted to the spot and incapable of movement, so I had no option but to observe that there were two planes, fighters or similar, coming at an angle towards us to cross diagonally in the direction of our stern, where they could see the Red Ensign. They circled once to satisfy themselves that it was the Red Ensign and not the Hammer and Sickle of the U.S.S.R. and, to our relief, departed.

There was much discussion about this incident, with everyone expressing the opinion that they were glad that it was a daytime encounter. What would have happened had it been dark, when the pilots would have had difficulty with identification? There was little or no breeze so our flag was not "flying" and therefore difficult to identify. We concluded that, had that been the circumstance of the encounter, bombing would have been a distinct possibility. Needless to relate, we were anxious to clear that area as speedily as possible.

Whilst in the Yellow Sea heading south towards Shanghai, the lunchtime peace was disrupted when the Boatswain burst into the saloon to announce that there was a split in the ship's hull such that he could see through the side plating in the area of number three hold. The saloon was cleared as if the ship was on the point of sinking. No shout of, "You go first, sir," just a headlong rush for the saloon door, each with the self-survival thought of "me first, and which way is landwards?"

There was indeed a split in the hull of the *Kingsmount*, in the area of a vertical run of welding through one length of plating. Assessing the situation it was felt that, as the plating above and below the area of damage was intact, there was no immediate concern that the damage would extend further.

A radio message was despatched to the Owners requesting instructions as to our further movements. We maintained our progress south and hoped that the good weather which we were experiencing would continue. The Deck Officers set about the task of examining all hull plating to ensure that similar fracturing was not present in other areas.

Eventually a message was received from London that we should set course for Ceylon and the port of Colombo, where a thorough hull inspection would be undertaken by Lloyds surveyors at Walker's Dockyard.

Arriving at that port the indicated inspection was carried out and it was confirmed that the split was an isolated incident which could be contained.

When work in this connection had been effected we were to continue in ballast and head for the Red Sea, through the Suez Canal and along the North African coast to the port of Bone in Algeria, where we would load a cargo for Antwerp in Belgium. After discharge we were to sail the ship to drydock at Rotterdam, at which port the entire crew would be "Signed off".

Although this news was well received, there was still some concern that, although Lloyds had cleared the ship as being seaworthy for the proposed voyage, further hull deterioration would result from the stresses which the long voyage would entail. Such thinking was not ill founded. What had happened to the hull of the *Kingsmount* was not a unique happening, there was ample evidence that many such ships had foundered when hull plating had split. Indeed, at that time an investigation was under way in the States to establish why this was happening and, as a consequence of this enquiry, a great many of one particular build of ship were being laid up pending the full results of the investigation.

As a matter of interest the enquiry was to find that the problem was a direct result of man's greed to short-change his employer. Many of certain of these wartime ships were built in sections outside what would be considered proper ship building controls; small engineering establishments with reasonable plating and welding facilities were contracted to provide large sections of hull, which were later assembled at a proper ship building location.

The investigation was to discover that, although the basic pay for Welders in the many yards providing such sections was pretty much the same, the take-home pay for welders at one particular yard was considerably higher than for other similar establishments.

Finally, after lengthy undercover work, it was established that Welders in the yard concerned had been cutting corners and not filling the designed plate chamfer with weld. Rather than building up weld within the chamfer as specified, welders had instead been filling the root area of the butted plate chamfers with rod and then welding over the top of that. The result of this chicanery was that the Welders earned an extraordinary level of pay. If I recall correctly, several Welders were sent to prison for this deceit. However, I consider this a small price to pay for possibly having caused the death of many seamen.

I say possibly caused death simply because those ships which did founder as a result of hull failure were never recovered to prove beyond reasonable doubt that defective welding was the sole reason for the loss of the ship. It should also be remembered that the German Navy supremacy (U-Boats) in the North Atlantic was such that the life expectancy for these ships was very low, one or two cross-Atlantic trips at most. Was such a high level of specification really necessary in the circumstances which prevailed? A poor argument, but one which was, I believe, offered in defence of those who had cut corners.

Chapter Thirteen

So what did I think of seafaring after such an experience? That first trip had taken me right around the world, something which many who have sailed for years never achieved. Outwards through the Panama Canal and back through the Suez Canal, that voyage took me from the river Elbe to the North Sea; then the English Channel and across the Bay of Biscay into the North Atlantic for North America.

From Norfolk, Virginia, down the Atlantic Ocean, through the Gulf of Mexico and the Caribbean Sea to the Panama Canal, through the Canal, out into the vast Pacific Ocean and across to Japan.

After Japan through the Sea of Japan, the Yellow Sea, the South China Sea, the Bay of Bengal to Ceylon and then into the Indian Ocean.

The Arabian Sea into the Gulf of Aden and then that hotbed the Red Sea which was to result in the introduction into the English Dictionary of the word POSH: *P*ort *O*ut-*S*tarboard *H*ome. Winds in that area of sea are usually in one direction, air conditioning had still to be invented, so those who could afford the cost booked passage in a cabin which would always assure them of some ventilation.

Through the Suez Canal and into the Mediterranean Sea and then through the Strait of Gibraltar to enter the Atlantic Ocean once again and finally home.

The social side of the voyage was limited in that, arriving in port, the Engineers had so much to attend to there was little energy for anything else – well, almost nothing else.

The Radio Officer was also Irish and hailed from Co. Wicklow. He was at that time in his early fifties and had been at sea for over thirty years. He was a giant of a man who considered drink to be a serious matter which should always be given full and undivided attention. Next to the drink, he enjoyed nothing better than a good "punch up" and had an uncanny knack of either becoming involved in, or as was more often the case, starting a fight.

He was unmarried, considering his finances only sufficient for one. Anyway, he had no intentions of settling ashore so why support a facility which he would seldom use? "A wife? sure, what would I do with a wife? Wouldn't she be restless with me away all the time? And you know, Donal, it's got to be fed, and it's too far from the ground to nibble the grass." Which statement was way above me in those early days, I simply laughed and left it at that.

Sparks was a one-off. He took me under his wing early on in the voyage and managed to get me involved in all manner of escapades which, on occasion, had me silently vowing that I would never go ashore with him again. However, his company soon became addictive and, try as I might, I could not ignore his request when he knocked on my cabin door, "Come on, Donal, let's get to hell off this rust tub and give the locals a treat."

He was amazed when he learned that I was still "intact", this at twenty-one years of age. "Are you all right?" he asked. "Do your bits work? Well, we will have to change all that. You must clear the dirty water from your system," he continued, "Should you not do so, sure your engine will rust up. You must keep it working, and training is essential if you are going to be any good. Fancy reaching for the gun one day only to find it rusty and unable to fire!" Again, much of what Sparks offered went past me.

Following this he had but one aim and this was that I should lose my cherry and that he should be the one to arrange for this to happen. Obviously I was unaware of his intentions in this regard and, whenever he knocked on my cabin door, I willingly joined him to go ashore and treat the locals as he put it.

My downfall came in Japan at one of the many Girl Houses which flourished in the port of Muroran; at that time such establishments were advertised in the town street plan as passed to each crew member by a Customs officer who lived aboard ship during the duration of our stay in port. Girl Houses were not indicated by name but were depicted as a pink blob in the street where they were located. The loss of my cherry occurred at one such establishment named the Midorie and was master-minded by Sparks who had enlisted another Officer to ensure that everything went according to plan; nothing was left to chance. Muroran was quite a large circular port and we were berthed at an Iron Foundry at a point opposite the town. At the opposite end of the wharf, on open land, was a detachment of American soldiers residing under canvas. They operated a ferry service across to the town at 6.00 p.m. each evening returning promptly at midnight and this service, we were informed, was available to us.

During dinner in the saloon one evening the Second Mate said that an English film was being shown that night in one of the local cinemas. "Is that a fact?" said Sparks, "no doubt there will be Japanese subtitles but they won't bother us. Are you going?" So it was agreed that the three of us should avail ourselves of the American army ferry service across to Muroran.

Arriving in town it was proposed that we should have a couple of drinks before we made our way to the picture house. With Sparks it was always a couple of drinks; as he said, "A bird can't fly on one wing."

So it was that we arrived at a hitherto unvisited, and what appeared to me as a rather strange, drinking establishment. At least, I was informed that it was a drinking establishment where we were welcomed and requested to take off and leave our shoes at the door. "Go through, Donal," said Sparks, pushing me forward into a room where several kimono-clad girls were sitting on rush matting.

At this point I was not unduly concerned, as such girls were always to be seen in any of the many drinking dens visited on previous trips ashore. Sparks, who appeared to have the ability to converse in any language, was deep in conversation with an older woman, after which he joined us suggesting that we should retire to another room where drinks would be made available.

The three of us were led by three girls to another small room, which contained nothing by a single mattress, when we had settled down a tray of drinks arrived. Although the beer was not too good we soon downed the three bottles and requested that another tray be provided.

The girls were very friendly. They could speak the odd word of English and great play was made when one of the girls sidled close to me and, taking my arm, started to point at the hands of my watch. She spoke to the other girls whilst pointing at the hands, telling them the time I thought. Turning to me the girl asked that I "say in English" whereupon I started to give her an English lesson.

Deeply engrossed as I was in doing my bit to foster relations between our two nations, I was unaware that the others had departed. She was young and beautiful, the atmosphere was scented and it seemed quite natural when she started to caress me.

As John Wayne said, "A man's got to do what a man's got to do", so it was that my cherry was lost to a young but highly experienced Japanese girl. Well, by my standard she was experienced; gentle and encouraging, she fully understood that I was unsullied and, who knows, maybe an event such as that rated high with such women. Later she departed the room to return a few minutes later with Sparks and the Second Mate.

They entered the room with knowing smiles on their faces – ''We know what you have done'' sort of thing. Putting his arm around me Sparks asked if it had been good. Changing your oil, he added was what it was all about. If God had invented anything better then He had kept it a secret.

We did go to the pictures that evening. However, my thoughts were elsewhere, although the event had not been earth-shattering; in fact, it had really been a non-event, I could think of nothing else but that lovely young girl who could not have been much more than sixteen. Already I was planning ways in which I might get Sparks to accompany me on a return visit. I was unsure of the way, and therefore was in need of his assistance.

I need not have bothered my head. It was as if he had read my thoughts and thereafter we were regular visitors to that establishment. Whereas he sampled many of the assorted wares on offer, I had eyes only for one maiden, my first love as it were, and come sailing day the thought that I would probably never see her again was quite unbearable.

All-knowing, Sparks sensed my feelings and endeavoured to point out in the nicest of terms that she was but a working girl. No matter what my feelings were towards her, as far as she was concerned I was just another ''trick''. He promised that there would be others just as fair in other ports. There were, but none compared with that first fumbling experience in that establishment in Muroran, Japan.

As I have said, Sparks was a one-off. I have met many what I would term ''characters'' through the years, but he towers head and shoulders above them all. He was most definitely unique and life was never dull when he was around; unpredictable yes, but never dull, a man's man who could cope in any situation and, as the saying goes, he could fight, fXXX, wheel a barrow or push a truck.

Whereas the rest of the Officers were employed by the shipowner, in that case the Capeside Steam Ship Company, Sparks, and indeed the majority of Radio Officers throughout the Merchant Service at that time, were employed by Marconi Marine. A Shipping Company in need of a Radio Officer simply contacted Marconi, who then directed one of their staff to join the ship in question.

The result of this was that Radio Officers were limited in the amount of money available to them through the normal shipboard channel. Prior to arriving in a foreign port the "Sub. List" would be passed around and we simply entered in sterling the amount of money we required to be made available to us. There was no limit to this, providing of course that your account with the owner was in the "Black". Upon arrival in port the Ship's Agent brought aboard the required amount of money in the local currency and we then signed for whatever we took.

I can't recall the limit of Sparks' account with that particular ship. Whatever it was, it was insufficient to his needs and early on in the voyage he had reached a point where there was nothing left to draw. The Captain, a Welsh puritan, or so he would have us believe, was not particularly taken with Sparks and his attitude to life, and as a result he would not allow him to draw money in advance of the due date.

This caused Sparks some inconvenience; although he could go to any Marconi Office across the world and draw money, this facility was rather limited in that offices were few and far between. Major ports such as New York, Rotterdam and Hong Kong presented no problem, but most of the ports we touched during that voyage were a problem, so there were regular arguments between him and the Captain.

However, Sparks usually won the day. The Captain had an old personal radio which was most unreliable and prone to failure, at which time he would ask if Sparks would have a look at it. "See what you can do with this, Sparks. I really miss the World News on BBC." Now, if he got Sparks on a bad day, the quick answer was, "I am employed to operate and service the ship's radio, not your personal possessions, SIR."; Or, "Why should I do you a favour when you treat me like a wayward child?" The Captain would depart knowing that he was never going to win.

Eventually the Captain would reach a point where he could not face another day without his beloved radio. He would enter the Radio Shack and, after passing the time of day and enquiring if there had been any messages, he would promise all manner of things if only Sparks would repair his radio. On the strict understanding that there would be no further problems with money, Sparks would then set about his repair task.

He was quite a genius with radios and always managed to return the instrument to the Captain in perfect working order. However, come the day when the Captain returned to his old ways, you could be sure of one thing, a few days later that radio would have a relapse and the now established routine would recommence.

I said that the Captain would have us believe that he was a saint. Certainly he never drank, nor did he smoke or swear. A good clean-living man, who frowned on those who sought the pleasures of the flesh. He always knew of a ship which had suffered several incidents of venereal disease following a visit to the port which we were about to enter. This was his way of warning the crew of the consequences of visiting the whorehouse – not the possible outcome, as he saw it, but a certainty that any such visit would result in syphilis at the very least.

Whilst in Muroran the Captain was to show that he was not as pure as he would have us believe.

One night, when Sparks and I were making our way to our usual haunt and, on the point of rounding a corner which brought us directly opposite the place we sought he pulled me back saying, "Stop, Donal, will you look there?" Looking across to the establishment I saw the Captain in the doorway bending down tying his shoe laces; standing beside him was the Madam.

Sparks for once was speechless, well almost, "Donal will you look at that dirty old bastard? What sort of man is he? He wants us to believe that he is as white as white, yet there he is fresh from an oil change himself." Seeing the Captain rising and preparing to depart, he cupped his hand around his mouth and shouted in his direction, "You dirty old bastard."

Turning on his heels Sparks hared off down the road and dodged into the first alleyway. I was right there with him, my heart pounding as I contemplated the consequence of such a foolish outburst. Sparks was Irish: once he opened his mouth his nationality was very obvious, he had a very deep voice and was at that time, I suspect the only person with such a voice for a thousand miles.

When I could speak, I asked why he had been so stupid. "The Captain will not be amused and will call us to his cabin when we return to the ship." "Ah, don't worry, Donal, he won't know who it was." In spite of my worry I burst out laughing and, seeing the funny side of his comment, Sparks shook with laughter fit to burst.

Obviously the Captain knew exactly who it was that had spotted him leaving a Girl House. However, he never spoke about the affair; his concern would be that Sparks kept this knowledge to himself. To this end his attitude towards Sparks altered and there were seldom, if ever, any more money problems.

Sparks and I shared the same table in the saloon where he sat opposite me and always had some comment to make in respect of the food. Although my mother kept a good table at home, food such as I was now experiencing was a completely new ball game. There was a menu for each meal, and there were at least three choices for each of the four courses.

My first sight of Sparks in action was at breakfast on morning, when the choice of starters included a small helping of curry and rice. I had never heard of curry and therefore had no idea of how it should be eaten – that is, did it require salt and pepper, or whatever? Hearing Sparks order curry, I thought right, I will stick with the smoked fish, observe his plate and, who knows, one day I may become more adventurous. When the curry arrived I was surprised to see that its consistency was not unlike stew; a different colour perhaps but it still looked like stew to my untrained eye.

Accepting the meal from the Steward, Sparks reached for the marmalade and proceeded to spoon a large helping onto the curry and mix the lot together. A right mess, I thought to myself, making a note never to attempt curry.

I was always quite happy with the meals in that there was always one of the course options which was acceptable. Obviously there were times when some of the courses on offer would not be my preference, but I never departed the saloon hungry.

Sparks was always complaining about the quality of the food – it was under-cooked, over-cooked, too small a portion, the left-overs from the previous meal tarted up and put into a pastry casing. Every day brought some complaint about the food and, as he never whispered, everyone present overheard his comments. Some would keep their heads down lest the Captain marked them down as other Sparks. Some, however, would agree with him, usually in whispers to ensure that the Captain did not hear.

One day when Sparks was sitting in my cabin I asked why he was forever complaining about the food, it was not so bad that constant complaint was necessary. I should not have bothered because his reply had me baffled. It was both true and false, but more truth than fabrication.

His contention was that, should one not complain about the quality of food, then the Chief Steward assumed that you were happy – that he was being successful in his endeavours and that at last, after long years of service, he had achieved the ultimate goal when all meals were acceptable.

Continuing, Sparks stressed that for some perverse reason Chief Stewards liked to be in a state of conflict with the crew over the quality and quantity of food which they made available; should they suddenly find that everyone was happy with their efforts then standards would be reduced such that complaints

were again heard in the saloon. He also held the belief that the owner's victualling allowance, so much per crew member per day, was not being adhered to;
the true victualling cost was considerably less than budget with the Captain and
the Chief Steward working a fifty:fifty fiddle with the savings. That being the
case, then in Spark's opinion, complaint was essential if standards were to be
maintained.

As with our departure from the U.K., our eventual return was to Euston
Station, London, this on a wet Sunday evening. A Company representative met
us and gave each sufficient money to see them home; although our contract
with the Ship Owner had been terminated on the Continent when we had
"Signed off", the balance of money due to each would be paid by cheque to
our respective homes. Each person was given a rail voucher to get them to their
home port, that is, everyone except Sparks; as ever he was flat broke.

The single fare at that time, Euston-Holyhead-Dublin, was about fifty-four
shillings, in today's coinage £2.70. Sparks, as stated, was broke and of course,
whilst Marconi would pay this fare, they were not at the station so he was, in a
way, stranded. I offered to buy his ticket, pointing out that he was due for a rest
and should make his way home. He would have none of this: "Ah, don't worry,
Donal, sure I will get another ship tomorrow." That was the last I saw of him;
however, I have thought of him often.

As he had said, many women were available through the years to come and I
was to visit many an "establishment' – not, I hasten to add, as a customer, but
simply to observe the set-up. In fact, myself and a later shipmate made quite a
hobby of seeking out these places and watching the comings and goings. In
some, the girls were young and even inviting. However, I soon realised that
what Sparks had said, when I was depressed at our departure from Japan, was
correct: they were business girls, and loved each customer only until the next
"trick" came along.

Some of these establishments were really rough and most would not partake
of what was on offer if given a gold clock. In particular I recall one such place in
Montevideo in Uruguay: this was not unlike a doctor's waiting room, where
customers sat around reading papers and magazines awaiting their turn. There
were rooms off the waiting room and, as a girl became available she would
shout, "Next", this whilst standing outside her door and attired in a wrap-over
dressing gown. Most definitely not an inviting place.

Also down the scale was the notorious Bull Ring at Basra in Iraq. The girls
were very young but, again, wild horses would not drag you to sample the
wares. As with the place at Montevideo, this was nothing but a whore house.

There were others which had a lounge bar atmosphere. One such was the Jardine Villa Rosa at Maracibo in Venezuela, a most pleasant establishment with a sizable dance floor and live music. The business girls there were of every shape, size and colour, a most extensive selection to suit every taste. The atmosphere was great. Most crews made their way to its doors and most, I would say, seldom if ever sampled the wares.

The girls were not pushy. If you wanted business that was fine. However, if you simply wanted to dance they would oblige and dance the hours away with you. At least they would dance until such time as a customer approached them, when they would depart to attend to business. Dancing around the floor was one way in which they could display their bodies to the assembled gathering, tempt the fence sitter into action and turn another "trick". Obviously rooms were available at the Villa Rosa where the girls did their business. These presumably were controlled by the owner and paid for each time they were used.

Less enticing were the bars which abounded in Skipper Street, Antwerp. As a general rule the women in these places were most uninviting and very crude. Not the sort of place to be recommended and certainly as far as I was concerned one visit along that street was sufficient.

At some ports the business girls sought out the customers and it was not unknown for them to knock on the cabin door and enquire if you wanted a "bed mate". As with those who worked the docks at Dublin, these "ladies of the night" had seen better days and were more or less reduced to begging.

Clearly these women were unable to compete in the business houses where the punter expected a reasonable quality of girl, so they became mobile and searched out the client. They knew that there were sailors who would never let it be known that, albeit infrequently, they did (as an old shipmate used to say) need an oil change.

They usually frowned when their mates stated quite openly that they were going ashore to "bag off", a much-used term meaning that they intended visiting a brothel. No, they sat aboard ship and some lived in hope that there would be a knock on their cabin door, this at a time when the occupants of adjacent cabins were ashore; they were a bit like wardrobe drinkers.

Chapter 14

The bad experiences as endured during my first voyage did nothing to dampen my enthusiasm that I wanted to make the Merchant Service my career. Certainly that trip had been a catalogue of disasters which would be attested to by all who had served in that particular ship, regardless of everything, I was still adamant that the sea and sailing offered all that I had ever desired, I had no interest beyond ships and shipping.

I reasoned that, having experienced and survived what was considered to be an exceptional voyage, the bottom of a trough as it were, then surely all future experiences must be better; that being the case then, my resolve was strengthened rather than weakened. So, after a short spell of leave in Dublin I set off once again for Liverpool, which, because of its proximity to Dublin, was to become my home port.

Those were the days when the competent marine engineer was in great demand and so could pick and choose the route he wished to sail, at times it might even be possible to pick the precise ship in which he wished to serve. Demand was such that at times the ''Situations Vacant'' columns of the *Liverpool Echo* carried several advertisements for marine engineers for ships that were either in, or due to arrive at Liverpool docks.

As the South American trade appealed to me I set about obtaining the detail of those Shipping Lines which catered for that trade. In a remarkably short space of time I had secured a suitable position aboard a passenger/cargo vessel which suited my requirement.

Whilst I enjoyed the meat trade, and that basically is what it was, general cargo to perhaps half a dozen South American ports and then frozen meat home, I soon tired of the set routine where we sailed at a specified time and date from one port to arrive at our next destination with the same preciseness. My choice was that whilst the outward destination was known at the time of the ship's departure, thereafter, our ports of call would be something of a mystery tour.

Tramping alone offered what I wanted, the regulated arrival and departure routine of many Shipping Lines simply did not attract me; on the contrary, the thoughts of sailing into the same ports month after month left me cold. Such trading was best suited to the married man who wished to be involved in the rearing of his family. Some sailing routes had seamen at home for a few days each month and so they could play an active part in family affairs.

Marriage at that time was the furthest thing from my mind; anyway, how could you expect to see the world when your sailing was limited to Liverpool–New York–Liverpool? No, tramping, although it could have its bad points, offered me a better chance to visit the exotic places which had beckoned me from an early age.

The remainder of my years in the Merchant Service were spent tramping, taking me to most countries of the world and in doing so pretty well satisfied my wanderlust; I could not have been happier; here I was, doing everything my heart had ever desired, and getting paid into the bargain.

In the early days the ships in which I served were crewed by Indian seamen where conditions were really superb. The manning levels in our accommodation were usually one crewboy to four Officers; our every need was catered for including the washing and ironing of our clothes.

Indian crews were most dependable. They seldom if ever drank intoxicants, so the problems which drink had caused during my first voyage never arose. They never went missing ashore and were always available for their watch-keeping duties; they were not as adept at their work as some other crews. However, the fact that they could be relied upon to attend to their allotted tasks was preferable to the increased but undependable skills of others.

Whether or not they were limited in their ability to tackle anything other than the job for which they had been employed is difficult to assess. Certainly they never impressed me that there was a willingness to step over the demarcation line and expand their job knowledge. It was as if they had an inborn single-mindedness which only allowed them to undertake their specified job, and this after extensive training.

They could master a situation where under a given set of circumstances they were required to open valve A and close valve B, and follow that routine day in day out. However, should it become necessary to alter that sequence, due to a changed set of conditions, then you could wrong-foot them and have all manner of problems. As a consequence of this limitation, crew numbers were higher than would be necessary with other crews. Of course their rates of pay were lower and, I suspect, victualling bills were also less, on balance therefore, the Ship Owner got the better deal with Indian crews, and a far higher degree of loyalty.

Indian crews, that is deck and engineroom ratings, had their own cooks, and their respective galleys were positioned either side of the stern accommodation. Each Friday the cooks would be issued with a week's ration of non-perishable food stuffs for each member of his department. Perishables such as meat, fish., etc., were issued daily.

Crew members had a system of eating whereby five men messed together and, through seven days the five would use only four men's rations of non-perishable food stuffs. The result of this self-imposed limitation was that each of the group could build up a sizable quantity of such food to take home with them at the end of their Contract.

To keep the cost of a crew change to a minimum, Shipping Companies always endeavoured to arrange that changes would be effected when a vessel was in the vicinity of India, if not in either Bombay or Karachi. Occasionally this was not possible and, their two-year service point being imminent when, if not discharged, wages would be increased by as much as fifty per cent, the Company would take the least expensive option and arrange for a crew change outside India.

On one such occasion, at the port of Ravenna in Italy, we were advised to prepare the crew for repatriation by charter flight to India. Each seaman, we were advised, was to be strictly limited in terms of their luggage weight and we were also advised that the responsibility to ensure compliance with the weight restriction would rest with the ship's officers.

As previously explained, each seaman had deprived himself through two years and not eaten the total of his non-perishable food rations, this in the knowledge that his self-denial would benefit his family. Also accumulated were a number of galvanised washing buckets, soap and soap powders, cleaning cloths, etc.; add to this purchases through the voyage in the many ports visited, in particular Paddy's Market in Liverpool, and it will be appreciated that each seaman's luggage was in excess of the weight limit.

All bags, bails, etc., were assembled on deck when we weighed the total of each man's luggage and advised the excess. You would have to experience such an occasion to fully understand and appreciate all that transpired through this ordeal, and ordeal it most certainly was. The men cried, "Sahib, I have saved this, my baby needs it," all manner of plea, until finally they became noticeably angry.

The scenes became quite heated, tempers flared and crew boys who had always been calm and obedient became very hostile. Although we were in agreement that the weight excess was the result of their self denial in that they did not use the total of their shipboard allowances, we had no alternative but to inform them that unconsumed stores were the property of the Shipping Company. We accepted that the stores had been issued to the men, however, the rations provided were in excess of the requirement, surplus and therefore belonged to the shipowner.

The only solution was for us to arrange for the excess to be transported separately to India at the men's expense, an unacceptable solution which the men rejected; so we set about examining each seaman's luggage to assess how the required weight reduction could be achieved with the least pain. With few exceptions the objective was arrived at without the need to relieve the men of their valuable non-perishable food rations, this due to the fact that the excess weight was mainly paint drums which were being used as packing cases, and galvanised washing buckets.

When the crew had departed and before the arrival of the replacement crew we inspected the accommodation to locate any messages which the departing seamen might have left for the new crew. Crew changes were always planned such that those arriving had no contact with the departing crew, this to ensure that wrangles were not exchanged. Had one crew managed to gain an advantage in whatever, it was important that this was unknown to the relief crew and that they start their term of service at the baseline. In time they would develop their own wrangles, at the onset, however, it was most definitely square one.

As far as the engineroom ratings were concerned our first task was to establish what, if any, experience each had of that particular type of ship. There were times when some members of the new crew were known to one or another of the officers; on such occasions our task would be relatively easy in that we knew the men's capability and that they were familiar with certain of the engine-room procedures.

Some, however, although known to us, would act dumb giving the impression that they had forgotten all previous training, as a consequence full training was necessary. This could be very trying, you could spend hours getting them to understand a sequence of operations as necessary for a certain set of circumstances only to find that you had achieved little or nothing.

Such training required great patience, in particular on diesel vessels when the engine exhaust was used to generate steam for the ancillary machinery; approaching port in such a vessel when the engine would be slowed or even stopped, the boilers were adjusted and instead of being fuelled by the exhaust they were fuelled by heavy oil. As a Junior Engineer and a Fireman effected this change the training of any inexperienced new crew members was the Junior's responsibility. The changeover, exhaust to boiler oil, was not too involved, however, I have seen Juniors spend several hours tutoring a Fireman only to find that come the real thing, the job was fluffed; on such occasions the air would be blue and many a Junior has threatened to use his Fireman as boiler fuel did he not get his act together.

It should be said that when training was completed the Indian seaman was most reliable and you could be assured that they would do exactly as required. However, I have seen very few who had wanted to do other than that for which they had been engaged; whatever rung of the ladder they were on was sufficient, there was no ambition beyond that point. Indeed some whom I have sailed with were on the bottom rung when I first met them, meeting up again some years later, they were still at the same level, level one; they were, however, very happy with their position and I suppose that such a mental state is to be envied, not criticised.

The lower echelons were not on watches but worked regular days in the engineroom on cleaning duties, etc. The bottom "floor" of a ship's engineroom is usually chequered steel plating which is kept spotlessly clean by continuous wiping with a cloth; I have seen a man wipe a cloth over the same square metre of flooring for hours; although their eyes were open I formed the opinion that they had the ability to "switch off", the body was most certainly there, in all other regards they were most definitely elsewhere, or so it appeared. At the first ring of the bell which indicated the end of the work period, or indeed any other such warning bell, they were immediately alerted, and hastily departed the engineroom.

I was to witness their ability to quickly vacate the engineroom when steaming up the Shat-el-Arab to Basra in Iraq one afternoon; it was perhaps 1630 hours and the full complement of day-work ratings were in the engine room. We were in a "Stand By" situation and steaming "Full Ahead", all was peaceful, as ever when nearing the end of the day-work shift period the ratings were all to be seen cleaning in the area of the exit, ready to act as soon as the bell rang.

However, minutes before that time the telegraph rang an urgent "Full Astern", this as the ship took a sudden list of perhaps forty degrees which resulted in my colleague and I sliding away from our stations towards the generators. Wondering what had occurred to cause our situation whilst at the same time attempting to grasp something for support I noted the last of the ratings ascending the stairs, we were very much alone.

Everything which happened occurred within a short space of time; the telegraph command became more urgent, repeatedly ringing "Full Astern". I was furthest away from the engine control point and looking around observed that my colleague was paying more attention to the exit than to the telegraph; I was not over excited about our position, we were below the waterline and unaware of what had happened to cause our situation. I quickly weighed up my position and vowed that, should my colleague make a dash for the deck, then he would have my footprints up his back.

The noise of the racing engine, this because the propeller was obviously partly out of the water and the incessant ringing of the telegraph spurred us to gain a position at the controls when I answered the telegraph and my colleague altered the controls putting the engine full astern as commanded. The vibrations were enormous, the ship shook through its entire length as it struggled to free itself from whatever situation, ever so slowly we could feel the ship move and knew that soon we would be on an even keel.

The cause of our running aground was a steering engine failure; by all accounts we had been at a point in the river which required a change of direction, at the crucial time, the rudder failed to respond to the helm with the result that the ship ploughed up the sandy river bank to halt with our bow among some date palms. They say that every incident has an element of comedy, this was no exception.

The Chief Officer, positioned as he was on the bow, had a bird's-eye view of events; it was a beautiful sunny afternoon and he was admiring the scenery when to his amazement, rather than negotiate a bend, the ship continued up the river bank. He was further surprised when several ratings rushed onto the forecastle and proceeded to depart the ship via the date palms; if the ship was about to sink then it was most definitely going to the river bottom minus them.

We did not sink nor was there any such danger, we stopped mid-river to effect repairs to the steering engine at which time a boat was lowered to bring the "Deserters" back aboard; repairs successfully completed we continued our passage to Basra.

On another occasion when in the St. Lawrence River, Cape Breton Island to Toronto, the ship in which I was serving was involved in a collision which was very frightening. Because of severe fog our Pilot decided that we should get out of the main shipping lane, drop anchor and wait for conditions to improve; it was approaching midnight.

Towards the end of my watch at about 0300 hours, a telephone call from the bridge informed me that as conditions had improved the River Pilot would shortly be calling for engine power; I made the necessary preparations and responded when the telegraph rang "Stand By". Shortly afterwards the telegraph rang "Half Ahead", we re-joined the shipping lane and were soon under weigh in the direction of Quebec City. At 0400 hours I was relieved when I departed the engineroom for a much-needed shower and of course some sleep.

I had no sooner gained my bunk when there was a fearful crash which left me in no doubt that we had collided with something; I jumped from my bunk, donned some clothing and headed for the open deck. As the impact had occurred astern of our accommodation I went in that direction in the hope that I would see what the problem was.

Although the fog had lifted slightly it was still dark, therefore visibility was poor; arriving at the ship's side I could hear voices above me and looking in that direction I realised that they were coming from the bow of the ship which had rammed us; my first thoughts were, which direction is landwards and how far will I have to swim to safety. The ship, which I guessed to be a large unladen bulk carrier, was by that time slowly sliding astern of us.

When the Pilot of this vessel thought that the ships had cleared he gave the order to drop anchor; sadly we had not cleared with the result that the anchor, together with several fathoms of anchor chain, descended onto the steel housing of our after accommodation. There were perhaps fifty crew boys in that accommodation at the time when perhaps half a ton of metal dropped on their roof, thankfully none were injured; however, the screams which assailed my ears from the area had me thinking otherwise.

We again anchored where we remained until daylight when an inspection was carried out before we proceeded to Montreal for cargo discharge and repairs. We had been very lucky, we could well have been holed and required to take to the lifeboats, also, the anchor could have killed somebody when it had dropped onto our poop, all in all we had a narrow escape and were well pleased that we had come out of the encounter so lightly.

When working on the Canadian Great Lakes, in particular when in the locks which allowed passage between the St. Lawrence River and Lake Erie, each ship had to provide the necessary manning to moor their ship in the lock. To this end ships working in the lakes were fitted with a special boom facility which allowed them to land four seamen off the quarters as the ship entered each lock.

This facility comprised a swinging boom to which was fitted a single seat; as the ship entered a lock the booms were swung outwards from each quarter to land a seaman holding one end of a mooring rope, onto the lock walling. Upon landing the seaman would place the ropes around mooring bollards and remain in that vicinity until the ship was ready to depart the lock at which time they would release the ropes, climb aboard the boom and be hoisted aboard the moving ship.

That was the general idea, release the mooring rope and when the slack had been pulled inboard, dash for, and quickly get into the boom seat and be hoisted aboard ship; however, as the ship was not moving getting into the boom seat was not so easy, as a consequence it was not unusual for some poor Lascar to miss the boom and be left standing on the lock side. On such occasions we would have to wait outside the lock where we would wait until the Lascar caught up with us.

Whilst on the Great Lakes and docked in Montreal in August 1961, I received a letter from the Irish Income Tax Office which took me back seven years to my time in the *City of Amsterdam*; in his letter the Taxman stated that I owed him some money and that I should forward same by return post. Yes, the Irish Fir had again surfaced in my life.

Nineteen fifty-four in Ireland was pre-Pay As You Earn (PAYE) with the result that the Taxman did not receive anything of my salary as earned during my service aboard the *City of Amsterdam*; when I departed that vessel and returned to tramping I owed the Irish Taxman some money. This situation really bothered and, like all honest citizens, I lay awake for seconds most nights pondering how, come the next port of call, I would write and ask the Taxman to forward his bill so that I could clear my debt and relieve my conscience, thus re-establishing a proper sleeping pattern.

The Irish Taxman's tenacity and powers of detection had to be admired, definitely MI5 calibre; not only had he trailed me to Canada, he had also identified my ship and rank and established my forwarding address in Montreal.

The Irish Taxman's demand was to arrive at a time when the English Taxman was expressing grave concern for £10,000 which a certain Irish tenor owed them. Given that situation, and after extensive consultation with my colleagues in the saloon, it was felt that I should respond to the Irish Taxman along the lines that it would appear that he was making a bigger song and dance than his counterpart in the U.K., and this for a fraction of what the tenor owed.

The sequel? There is none. My letter, I suspect, hit the bull because I heard nothing further and – I still own that few quid plus interest, of course.

The opening of the Canadian Seaway afforded ocean-going ships the opportunity to traverse the Great Lakes and dock at such previously inaccessible ports as Duluth in Minnesota, or Superior in Wisconsin, both ports in the U.S.A., as well as Fort William and Port Arthur in Ontario, Canada. These four ports are situated at the extreme western edge of Lake Superior, the largest of the Great Lakes.

Wherever possible in the area of the many locks which made the rise to Lake Superior possible, this to a height of 612 feet above sea level, the local authority had erected stands adjacent to the locks where spectators could observe the passing ships. Indeed, did you tune your radio to the local radio station, you would hear it announced that ships of every nation passed through the locks daily, some stations even quoting statistics of the passing ship traffic.

These viewing stands were similar to football stadium stands and spectators arrived with packed lunches and spent the day observing the activity. At some locks, where there were no viewing stands, spectators simply lined the lock sides where they had bird's eye view of events, in particular, of crew members' cabins.

Emerging from the engineroom, Engineers would enter the shower room, undress, take a long refreshing shower and then, stark naked, cross the short distance to their cabins to get dressed. On several occasions I have entered my cabin in my "nookey suit" to find faces peering through the portholes. I don't know who had the greatest shock in these "sightings", the spectators or myself; however, such happenings were most unwelcome and gave me an inkling of how the animals in the zoo must feel.

Whilst on the Lakes the usual routine was to load a full cargo of grain at any one of the Lake Superior ports and take this down to Halifax in Nova Scotia. Following discharge we would sail to Cape Breton Island and the small port of Little Narrows, where we would load a cargo of gypsum for one of the Lake ports.

Occasionally we took our grain cargo to South America: Maracaibo, Cumana or La Guaira in Venezuela and after discharge we proceed in ballast to Georgetown (Demerara) where we would load bulk sugar for one of the Lake ports.

Come the end of the season, when the lakes would freeze over, we would lift our final cargo to Venezuela and after discharge make our way to New Orleans where we would load grain for some European port.

It was precisely such a trip which brought my seafaring to an early conclusion this in March 1962, ten years to the month after my departure from Dublin.

My seagoing career was terminated on the advice of our doctor who was concerned for my wife's health; not unlike many other wives she worried that, did a letter not arrive a few days after my due date at some foreign port, then my ship had been lost with all hands. That concern, coupled with what we now know must have been the onset of Multiple Sclerosis, was having a debilitating effect on her health such that I heeded the doctor's advice, swallowed the anchor and set about carving a career on dry land, far removed from that which I had intended.